The Knitting Man(ual)

THE KNITTING
Man(ual)

20+ PROJECTS FOR GUYS

Kristin Spurkland

Photographs by John Valls

TEN SPEED PRESS
Berkeley | Toronto

Ten Speed Press
PO Box 7123
Berkeley, California 94707
www.tenspeed.com

Distributed in Australia by Simon and Schuster Australia, in
Canada by Ten Speed Press Canada, in New Zealand by South-
ern Publishers Group, in South Africa by Real Books, and in
the United Kingdom and Europe by Publishers Group UK.

Jacket and text design by Betsy Stromberg
Makeup by Trish Grantham

Library of Congress Cataloging-in-Publication Data

Spurkland, Kristin, 1968–
  The knitting man(ual) : 20+ projects for guys /
Kristin Spurkland.
      p. cm.
  Summary: "Twenty-plus knitting patterns for men's clothing
and accessories featuring a range of projects for knitters of all
skill levels and reflecting a contemporary urban aesthetic"—
Provided by publisher.
  ISBN 978-1-58008-845-9 (alk. paper)
  1. Knitting—Patterns. 2. Men's clothing. I. Title.
  TT825.S7133 2007
  746.43'2041—dc22
                                        2007012435

Printed in China
First printing, 2007

1 2 3 4 5 6 7 8 9 10 — 11 10 09 08 07

CONTENTS

ACKNOWLEDGMENTS

Thank-yous to all the following people:

For their help in completing the knitting in the book: Nancy Atwood, Anne Berk, Lucinda Bingham, Sandy Bingham, Jamie Guinn, Stephanie Smith, Donna Warnell, and Jesse Stenberg (extra props to Jesse for modeling some of the finished clothing and for being the hand model in the technique photos).

For their fabulous modeling talents: Christopher Becker, Leon "Bing" Bingham, Gavin Bowes, Eric Dickerson, Kalen Garr, Anton Hougardy, Todd Jackson, Aiden Sanders, Anthony Schatz, Patrick Shearer, Lars Spurkland, and Tobben Spurkland. You're all lovely—and snappy dressers, too.

For talking to me about their knitting lives: Leon "Bing" Bingham, Don Cameron, Jay Petersen, Jan Spurkland, and Jesse Stenberg.

For helping me to make the book I dreamed of a reality: my editor, Julie Bennett; Trish Grantham for hair, makeup, and impromptu modeling; Betsy Stromberg for her book design; and John Valls for his beautiful photography.

Double thanks to Jan Spurkland, my brother, for his suggestion several years ago that I write a book of patterns for men, and to Jesse Stenberg, for suggesting the title when I was stuck.

Thanks to all of the Portland, Oregon, businesses that let us shoot on location: Concordia Coffee House, Frock, Hi-iH, Kennedy School, Redbird Studios, and Tonalli's Donuts; and Anton, Gavin, and Tony for letting us invade their home with lights, cameras, and wardrobe in tow.

INTRODUCTION

The history of knitting is not definitive. The oldest known pieces of knitted fabric date back to the fourteenth century in Europe and Egypt, although some sources cite an Egyptian sample from as early as the twelfth century. Although even older fabrics similar to knitting existed, these forerunners were probably created with a single threaded needle, a technique called *nålebinding*.

How this single-needle technique morphed into modern knitting is uncertain. One theory is that fishermen of the High to Late Middle Ages modified existing needlework techniques in the construction of fishing nets, eventually creating knitting as we know it today. As the fishermen sailed across the globe, they took their new needle craft with them, transmitting it around the world. Another theory is that knitting developed out of medieval Islamic cultures, moving into Europe via Africa and Spain and the Catholic missionaries who traveled those countries.

While its development and early history are unclear, we do know that by the mid-sixteenth century knitting had become a full-fledged industry with guilds, apprentice programs, and schools. People across Europe were employed in the knitting cottage industry, primarily outputting socks and stockings for the wealthy classes.

Surprisingly, these early knitting professionals were unquestionably men. Women and children eventually took up the trade, but in the beginning, knitting was a strictly male endeavor and remained so until the Industrial Revolution mechanized production. While both men and women followed knitting into the factories, hand knitting at home began its transformation into a feminine art. This is not to say that in the post–Industrial Revolution era men gave up knitting altogether. Sailors, farmers, and fishermen from many cultures continued to knit as a way to help the family or simply to keep clothes on their backs. Periodically, outside forces would push men back into knitting.

During World War II, many men knit in support of the war effort, making mittens, hats, and socks for the Army and Navy forces. In my days as a yarn shop employee, I meet a gentleman who had learned to knit in childhood, eventually utilizing his knitting skills during World War II repairing and knitting socks when need and opportunity arose. When I knew him, he was knitting "for his heart"—as a stress reduction exercise at

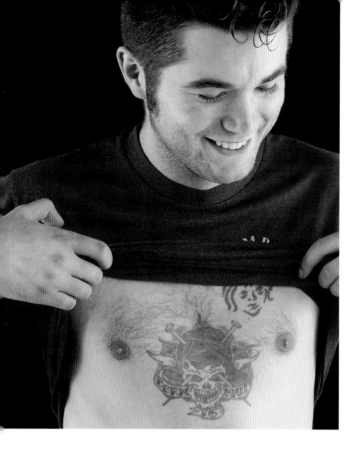

his doctor's suggestion. Historically men have knitted for a variety of reasons—to earn a living, to help their families, to support their country's soldiers, for their health—but what brings men to knitting today? I surveyed some male knitters for answers.

Jesse Stenberg, 24, who now teaches knitting classes and has done production knitting for knitting books (including this one), learned "as a joke" when he was 17. To his surprise, Jesse found he really liked knitting. "It gives me something productive to do while watching sports on TV." When he was 19, Jesse proved just how dedicated he was to the craft by getting the phrase *Born to Knit* tattooed across his chest, complete with modified skull and crossbones.

In 2006, Jesse taught a beginning knitting class for men. Two of his students were Don Cameron, 52, and Leon "Bing" Bingham, 72. Don and his wife, Darcy, own Knit/Purl, a yarn shop in downtown Portland, Oregon, so Don's motivation to learn was driven by his desire to understand more about the business and to be able to better help his customers. Bing wanted to make a hat for his soon-to-be-born grandson. Both men have continued to knit long after the class ended and the initial projects were completed.

My brother Jan, 29, learned to knit in the ninth grade as part of a class project in which students were asked to learn a traditional skill. He made a hat that was, in his words, "oversized, full of holes, and unwound itself in about two weeks. That didn't stop it from becoming a gift for a girl-friend, however." The joy of giving handmade gifts is frequently cited by the men I spoke to as one of their primary motives for knitting. "There is a large amount of pride that goes with giving handknit gifts," says Jan. "People's expectations of male knitters seems to be rather low, making almost any gift an instant success."

Jay Petersen, 48, remembers being fascinated by the cables in an afghan as a child, trying to figure out how they were constructed. "I like the architecture of knitting," he says. A knitter since he was 8 years old, Jay's interest is in nonfunctional knitting. "I'm more interested in the fabric…I like designing and knitting stitch patterns." While Jay does make garments, mostly seamless projects worked in the round, his primary interest is in the creation and execution of the stitch pattern

itself. He says, "I'm truly obsessed in that I think of knitting structures all the time."

How do men knit? The stereotype is that men are less likely than women to follow a knitting pattern. I found that (just as with women), there are degrees of adherence, interpretation, and total disregard of patterns, depending on the knitter. "Patterns are just starting points for a project. They are full of great hints, but to take full credit for something you make, you have to tweak it at least a little bit," says Jan. Dan "just makes things up." And Jay modifies existing patterns to suit his needs, often adapting flat construction to circular knitting. "I try to follow patterns," says Bing, but "execution is sometimes lacking." That's an experience all knitters can relate to. As Bing says, "Knitting is definitely not gender specific."

■   ■   ■

How did I come to write a book of patterns for men? The seed for *The Knitting Man(ual)* was planted during the very first knitting class I taught. I had three students, one of whom was an excellent knitter named Carl. During class, Carl told me about his difficulty finding appealing patterns for men's garments. As a result, he mostly knitted for his wife and child rather than himself. I count many male knitters in my circle of family and friends, and most share Carl's wish for more knitting options. I hope that *The Knitting Man(ual)* is a step toward fulfilling that need.

You may notice the words *classic, traditional,* and *vintage* showing up frequently in the pattern descriptions. Many designs in *The Knitting Man(ual)* are based on traditional styles and silhouettes, but interpreted with modern colors and construction. I drew on knitting traditions because I wanted to create sweaters and accessories that men would actually want to wear (rather than what women think men should wear), and it seemed the best way to achieve that was to look to the classics.

The Knitting Man(ual) includes designs with Scandinavian roots and vintage inspirations, but with a contemporary twist.

The patterns in *The Knitting Man(ual)* can of course be knit, and in most cases, worn, by either men or women. But it was my intention to create a book especially for all those bold and creative men stepping out of their expected rolls (as the receivers of hand-knit items) and taking things into their own hands to become the creators of the knits themselves.

TECHNIQUES

No manual would be complete without some technical information. If you are a beginner and need more basic information, check out the many knitting references available at your local yarn shop or bookstore. You can also find knitting instruction online—www.knittinghelp.com is a good place to start. The site features lots of how-to information, good instructional photos, and even some videos of various knitting techniques. The best way to learn to knit is probably from another knitter, so consider taking a class at a yarn shop or craft store or sitting down with a knitting friend and having him or her show you the basics.

Common Knitting Terms Defined

Here is a list of terms that show up frequently in knitting patterns, often without definition or explanation.

DOUBLE STRANDED YARN

(Also "holding two strands together as one," "with two strands of yarn held together," or "with yarn double stranded.")

This is simply knitting with two strands of yarn simultaneously, holding them together and treating them as if they were a single strand. Double stranding is done for a variety of reasons. I double stranded the yarn on the Saturday Morning Slippers (see page 29) to create a tweedy effect and a firm, sturdy fabric. For the Seaweed Throw (see page 25), the yarn I selected was too fine on its own (the motifs looked wimpy and didn't pop), but because it was otherwise perfect I opted to double strand the yarn to achieve a heftier gauge.

FASTEN OFF

This simply means to secure your yarn end after binding off or otherwise finishing a piece of knitting. Some people fasten off by threading the yarn end through the last stitch worked, while others prefer to just weave the end in securely. You can fasten off however you like, as long as you keep your yarn ends from unraveling.

GARTER STITCH

This is probably the first stitch pattern most knitters learn. How many of us started our knitting careers with a garter stitch scarf? Garter stitch looks the same on both sides (bumpy ridges running horizontally across the fabric), and doesn't curl (like many other stitch patterns). For that reason it is frequently used as a border pattern. When knitting back and forth on two needles, garter stitch is created by knitting every row. When working in the round (on a circular needle), garter stitch is created by knitting one round, then purling one round.

KNITWISE (kwise)

Usually used in reference to slipping stitches, knitwise simply means "as if you were going to knit." If you are instructed to "slip a stitch knitwise" it means that you insert your needle into the stitch as if to knit, then transfer the stitch from the left to right needle without actually knitting the stitch. *See also* **Purlwise**

PURLWISE (pwise)

Usually used in reference to slipping stitches, purlwise simply means "as if you were going to purl." If you are instructed to "slip a stitch purlwise" it means that you insert your needle into the stitch as if to purl, then transfer the stitch from the left to right needle without actually purling the stitch. *See also* **Knitwise**

RIGHT SIDE (RS)

This is the outside, or "public" side of a piece of knitting, and is not to be confused with the right-hand side of your work. Usually this distinction will be clear. Anytime you see the abbreviation "RS," you can be sure that the writer means the outside of the knitting. *See also* **Wrong Side**

SELVEDGE

Selvedge stitches are the stitches at either end of a knitted row. Usually selvedge refers specifically to the first and last stitches of the row; however, it can also refer to the entire side edge of the knitting. Context should make this distinction clear.

STOCKINETTE STITCH (St st)

This is the most common stitch pattern, and what most people think of when they think of knitting. Stockinette stitch has a distinct right and wrong side, and it will curl if no border is added. It is the foundation of most other stitch patterns. When working stockinette stitch back and forth on two needles, knit one row, then purl the next row. Repeat these two rows. When working stockinette stitch in the round (on a circular needle), knit every round.

WITH YARN IN BACK (wyib)

This means that the working yarn (the yarn you are currently knitting with) should be held at the back of your work, which is the same position you have it in when working knit stitches. Note that the back of the work is not necessarily the wrong side of the work. The back of your work is the side facing away from you *in the current moment* as you work the row. *See also* **With Yarn in Front, Wrong Side**

WITH YARN IN FRONT (wyif)

This means that the working yarn (the yarn you are currently knitting with) should be held at the front of your work, which is the same position you have it in when working purl stitches. Note that the front of the work is not necessarily the right side of the work. The front of your work is the side facing you *in the current moment* as you work the row. *See also* **With Yarn in Back, Right Side**

WRONG SIDE (WS)

The inside of a piece of knitting. *See also* **Right Side**

Getting Started

Here are some of my preferred methods for casting on, increasing, decreasing, and so on, as well as explanations of techniques used in the book that may not be familiar.

CAST ON

You probably already know at least one cast-on technique. I have included directions for the long-tail cast on (also called the Continental or slingshot cast on) because it is my hand's-down favorite. It is attractive, flexible, and once you get the hang of it, quick and easy to do.

1. Measure out a length of yarn—about $3/4$" for every stitch cast on is a good place to start. For example, if you want to cast on 100 stitches, measure a tail 75" long. Fine yarn will require a shorter tail, bulky yarn a longer tail. When in doubt, err on the side of too much tail. You can always cut off the excess.

2. Once you have measured the tail (don't cut it off!) make a slipknot at the skein end of the tail and place the knot on your needle. Hold the needle in your right hand, and make a "V" with your left thumb and index finger. The tail end of the yarn goes from your needle over your left thumb, and the ball end of the yarn goes from the needle over your left index finger. Keep tension on the yarn ends by holding them with your other fingers. (See photo A on page 8.)

3. Insert the needle up into the thumb loop (see photo B on page 8). Pivot the needle toward the index finger loop, inserting it into the loop from back to front (see photo C on page 8). Bring this loop through the loop on your thumb, releasing the yarn and pulling on the ends gently to tighten the stitch (see photo D on page 8). Repeat until you have cast on the desired number of stitches.

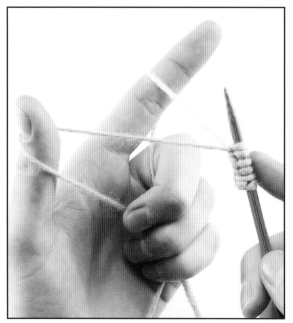

A. Proper hand position for casting on

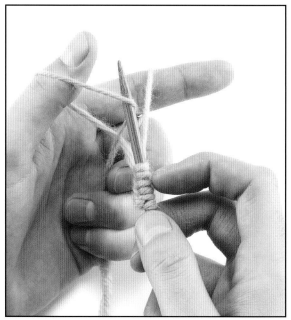

B. Insert needle into thumb loop

C. Insert needle into index finger loop

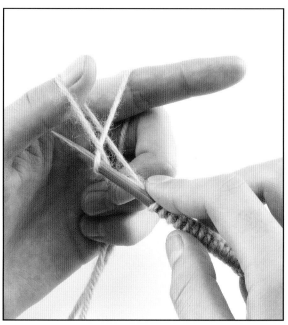

D. Bring index finger loop through thumb loop

BACKWARD LOOP CAST ON

This is a useful technique for casting on a few stitches in the middle of a project, such as on the Modern Aran Sweater (see page 101). For casting on at the start of a project, I prefer the long-tail method.

To make the backward loop cast on in the middle of a row or round: wrap the working yarn around your left thumb, so that it is traveling from the right-hand needle around the back of your thumb, across the front of your thumb, and down your palm (see photo A at right), where your fingers can grab it and pull it taut. Insert the right needle into this loop you've created and tighten down gently (see photo B bottom right). Repeat until you have cast on as many stitches as needed.

It may seem awkward at first, but with just a little bit of practice this cast on becomes very fast.

Working the Project

KNIT THROUGH THE BACK OF THE LOOP (ktbl)

You'll find a lot of this in this book. Knitting through the back of the loop twists the stitch, adding visual texture and firming up the fabric. It also tidies and stabilizes ribbing.

To knit through the back of the loop, insert the right needle tip into the back of the stitch, then complete the stitch as usual (see photo A on page 10).

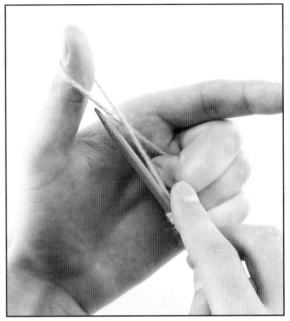

A. Proper hand position for backward loop cast on

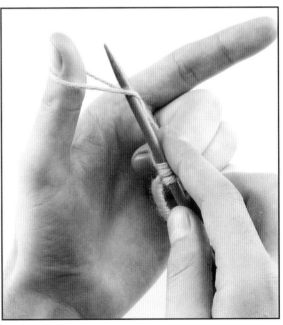

B. Insert the right needle into the loop

PURL THROUGH THE BACK OF THE LOOP (ptbl)

To purl through the back of the loop, insert the right needle tip into the back of the stitch, from left to right, then complete the stitch as usual (see photo B below).

A. Knitting through the back of the loop

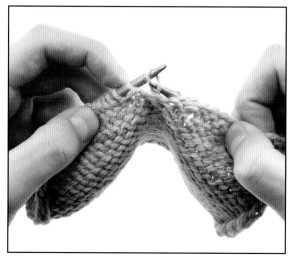

B. Purling through the back of the loop

SLIPPING A STITCH (sl)

Slipped stitches are used when decreasing, to create textural and color patterns, and to create tidy selvedges. To slip a stitch, insert the right-hand needle into the first stitch on the left-hand needle, then transfer this stitch to the right-hand needle without working (knitting or purling) it.

Your pattern should specify whether you are to slip the stitch knitwise (see page 6) or purlwise (see page 6). If your pattern is unclear, here's the general rule: when slipping stitches as part of a decrease, slip knitwise; in all other circumstances, slip purlwise.

Increases

Increases add stitches to your existing piece of knitting. There are many ways to increase, and the information below is in no way comprehensive. Rather, it includes the techniques I use for the projects in this book.

KNIT INTO THE FRONT AND BACK OF A STITCH (kfb)

This is my favorite increase technique. It's not invisible—but really, none of them are—but it's attractive and easy to do, and it doesn't leave holes in the fabric or look sloppy.

Knit the next stitch as usual, but leave it on the left needle. Pivot the right needle around to the back of the same stitch, and knit into the back of it. You have made two stitches out of one.

YARN OVER (YO)

A yarn over is a decorative increase. When worked alone, each yarn over adds a stitch to your fabric. When paired with a corresponding decrease, yarn overs add a decorative element.

To yarn over between two knit stitches: bring the yarn forward between the two needles, then back over the right needle. Knit the next stitch as usual.

To yarn over between two purl stitches: take the yarn back over the right needle, then forward between the two needles. Purl the next stitch as usual.

Decreases

Decreases reduce the number of stitches in your existing piece of knitting. There are many ways to decrease, and the information below is in no way comprehensive. Rather, it includes the techniques I use for the projects in this book.

DOUBLE DECREASE

A double decrease reduces three stitches down to one stitch. There are several double decrease techniques to choose from, but this is my favorite. The single stitch remaining after the decrease is centered between the two eliminated stitches, giving this decrease a vertical look rather than a left or right slant.

Slip the next two stitches together knitwise, knit the next stitch, then pass the slipped stitches over the knit stitch and off the needle. This is abbreviated as: Sl 2 tog kw, K1, p2sso.

SINGLE DECREASES

All of the decreases explained below reduce two stitches down to one. Some are worked over knit stitches, some over purl stitches. The primary difference is in the way the decreases slant. Some slant to the right, some to the left. Why does this matter? When shaping necklines and armholes, it's always nice to use "full fashioning," meaning that the decreases mirror each other on each side of the body. So when shaping armholes, you might work a Slip Slip Knit decrease (which slants left) at the beginning of the row, while at the end of the row you work a Knit 2 Together decrease (which slants right).

Some people prefer to place the right-slanting decrease at the beginning of the row and the left-slanting decrease at the end. This is purely a matter of preference (or may be dictated by the stitch pattern if it is more complicated than a simple stockinette stitch); try both options and go with what appeals to you. The point is to pair your decreases so they mirror each other. Below is a list of options to help you do so.

KNIT 2 TOGETHER (k2tog)

Right-slanting decrease.

Knit two stitches together as one.

KNIT 2 TOGETHER THROUGH BACK LOOP (k2tog tbl)

Left-slanting decrease.

Knit two stitches together as one, inserting the needle into the back of both stitches rather than the front (see photo A on page 12).

A. Knitting two together through the back of the loop

PURL 2 TOGETHER (p2tog)

Right-slanting decrease.

Purl two stitches together as one.

PURL 2 TOGETHER THROUGH BACK LOOP (p2tog tbl)

Left-slanting decrease.

Purl two stitches together as one, inserting the needle into the back of both stitches from left to right (see photo B below).

SLIP SLIP KNIT (ssk)

Left-slanting decrease.

Slip the next two stitches knitwise (see page 6) one at a time, then insert the left needle into the front of the stitches on the right needle and knit the slipped stitches together.

Special Techniques

READING CHARTS

Several projects in *The Knitting Man(ual)* include charts. Charts are a tool for depicting a color or texture pattern graphically, and are used as an alternative to lengthy written instructions. Here's a primer on how to read them.

1. Each box of the chart represents one stitch. Inside each box is a symbol or color indicating how that particular stitch should be worked. You'll find a key next to the chart explaining the meaning of the various colors and symbols used in the boxes.

2. Each row of the chart corresponds to one row of knitting. Row 1 on the chart is a graphic

B. Purling two together through the back of the loop

presentation of your actual first row of knitting. Row 2 depicts your second row. When knitting your third row, you should be looking at the "row 3" line of your chart. If you're looking at "row 6," something has gone wrong!

3. Charts are almost always read from bottom to top, starting in the lower right-hand corner—just the opposite of how we read text.

4. If the chart is for a project worked back and forth, the first row starts on the right-hand side, the second row starts on the left, the third on the right, the fourth on the left, and so on. For projects worked in the round on circular needles, every round starts at the right-hand side.

5. Occasionally you will come across a chart that deviates from this standard format. A good way to tell where you should start the row is to look for the row number at the side of the chart. If the number is on the right-hand side, start the row there. If it's on the left, start there. If there is no number (not uncommon, as many charts number alternate rows only), you'll have to rely on your logic, experience, and good sense to figure things out.

6. What tends to trip knitters up are unfamiliar terms listed on charts, such as "repeats" and "edge" or "balance" stitches. Let's break down these terms using the chart for Dad's Sweater. Note the bracket labeled "6 st rep." This means you will repeat those 6 bracketed stitches, and those 6 stitches only, over and over as you move across the row. When you get near

Dad's Sweater Chart

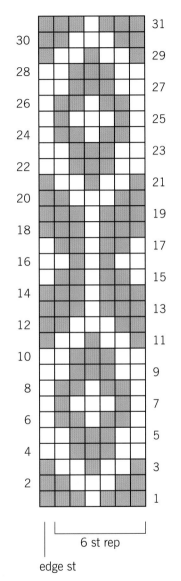

Indigo (A)

Oatmeal (B)

Odd-numbered rows are RS rows.

The edge st is worked at the end of RS rows, and at the beginning of WS rows.

This chart does not include the selvege sts worked at the beginning and end of every row (see Notes on page 44).

6 st rep

edge st

the end of the row, you won't have enough stitches remaining to work another full 6 stitch repeat. This is where your edge (or balance) stitches come in. Edge stitches are stitches at the beginning and/or end of the row that keep the pattern symmetrical—hence the term *balance*. In our example, if the row just stopped at the end of the 6 stitch repeat, the last repeat of the motif would be incomplete. The edge stitch completes the final motif. So edge stitches are worked at the beginning and/or end of the row only, and are not repeated across the row.

7. Here's the last bit of detail to comprehend (pay attention, because this one confuses a lot of people). Typical chart instructions might read as follows: "work through rows 1–66 of chart 5 times" (from the Seaweed Throw, page 25). This means: work across row 1, following the directions for working across the row as explained above. After completing row 1, you will go on to row 2, then to row 3, and so on, until you complete row 66. Once you complete row 66, you have worked rows 1–66 one time. You now need to repeat the entire process 4 more times.

Still confused? Your best bet is to consult a knitting friend with chart-reading experience, or talk to the people at your local yarn shop. They should be able to clarify it all for you.

STRANDED KNITTING

This is the color technique used for Scandinavian or Fair Isle knitting. The easiest method for those who are new to stranded knitting is the

A. Stranded knitting: Color A (indigo) travels above color B (oatmeal)

B. Wrong side of stranded knitting showing long floats

C. Intarsia interlocks

"pick up and drop" method. It isn't the fanciest two-color technique, but with practice it can be quite speedy, and the evenness of tension it provides is unsurpassed, especially when working across purl rows.

Here's how it's done (directions are written as if color A is the background color, and color B is the pattern color): knit color A for the number of stitches indicated in the pattern, drop it, pick up color B from under color A, knit as indicated in the pattern, drop B, pick up A from over color B, etc.

Always pick up color A from over color B, and color B from under color A. If you switch around, your yarns will get twisted, and the surface of your knitting will be uneven. The rule is that the background color (A) travels over the pattern color (B) (see photo A on page 14).

To keep your yarns from tangling around each other, put one skein on one side of your body and the other skein on the other side. The rule here is that the background color goes on your right side, while the pattern color goes on your left. Don't switch positions of the yarn—doing so will change the tension on the outside of the knitting. If you do this correctly, the yarns will never get twisted.

One more point: it is important to leave the "floats" (the strands of the color not in use that travel along the inside of your knitting) sufficiently long (see photo B on page 14). If the floats are too short, the surface of your knitting will pucker. Gently stretching your knitting down the right-hand needle before changing to a new color ensures that the floats will be long enough to span the distance they must cover.

INTARSIA

Intarsia is a technique for creating blocks of color in a knitted piece. Unlike stranded knitting, the second color is not carried across the entire width of the fabric; instead it is worked in an isolated area. A separate skein of yarn is used for each color block.

When its time to change from one color to the next, you need to do a step called "interlocking" to prevent gapping where the colors change.

To interlock: knit the last stitch with the old color. Pick up the new color from underneath the old color so that the yarns twist around each other, and proceed with the new color (see photo C on page 14). To prevent the stitches on either side of the interlock from distorting, give both the new color yarn and the old color yarn a tug after working the interlock.

I-CORD

I-cord is actually a narrow tube that is most frequently used for ties and drawstrings. You will need two double-pointed needles to make the cord. Cast on the desired number of stitches onto a double-pointed needle. *Knit the stitches, then, without turning your work, slide the stitches back to the right end of the needle. Repeat from * until the I-cord is the desired length. Bind off the stitches.

Finishing Up

GRAFTING

Also called kitchener stitch, grafting is most frequently used to join the toe stitches on socks. The technique is not difficult, but it does take concentration, so save your grafting for a time when you can work without interruption.

1. Place the stitches to be grafted on two needles. Hold these needles parallel in your left hand, with the wrong sides of the knitting facing each other. Thread yarn through a tapestry needle.

2. Bring the yarn through the first stitch on the front needle as if to purl. Leave this stitch on the needle. Bring the yarn through the first stitch on the back needle as if to knit, leaving this stitch on the needle.

3. Bring the yarn through the first stitch on the front needle as if to knit, and drop this stitch from the needle. Bring the yarn through the next stitch on the front needle as if to purl. Leave this stitch on the needle.

4. Bring the yarn through the first stitch on the back needle as if to purl, and drop this stitch from the needle. Bring the yarn through the next stitch on the back needle as if to knit, leaving this stitch on the needle.

5. Repeat steps 3 and 4 until all stitches have been grafted.

PICKING UP STITCHES

With the right side of your work facing you (unless instructed otherwise), insert your needle under an edge or selvedge stitch (see page 6) from front to back, wrap your working yarn as if to knit, and pull the loop through (see photo A at right).

SEAMING

Some instruction books give directions for starting your seams with a knot securing the seaming yarn to your fabric. I don't do this, as once a knot is tied, you can't adjust the seam yarn from the knotted end. I prefer to leave both ends free until I have completed the seam, so I can make adjustments at either end of the seam.

A. Picking up stitches

B. Proper seaming technique

When you are sewing a seam, insert the needle under the bars between columns of stitches (see photo B on page 16) and always insert the needle back into the fabric in the same place it exited from previously. This will ensure that you sew a straight seam, without any jogs or wavering lines.

SHOULDER SEAMS

Lay the pieces right side up, with the edges to be seamed adjacent to each other, one above the other (so the edges to be seamed will be horizontal as you look at them). Thread yarn through a tapestry needle. Starting at the right-hand edge of the seam, take the needle under the first stitch below the bind off from the lower piece, then under the first stitch below the bind off on the upper piece. *Take the needle under the next stitch under the bind off on the lower piece, then under the next stitch under the bind off on the

upper piece. Repeat from * until you have completed the seam (see photo C below).

SIDE AND SLEEVE SEAMS

Lay the pieces right side up, with the edges to be seamed side by side. Thread yarn through a tapestry needle. Insert the needle under the horizontal bar that runs between the selvedge stitch and the next stitch in. Pull the yarn through, then insert the needle under the corresponding bar on the other piece. Repeat up the length of the seam, alternating from side to side and pulling the yarn tight every inch or so (see photo D below). When seaming light to medium weight pieces, insert the needle under two bars at a time; for heavy weight pieces, stick to one bar. Be careful not to pull the seaming yarn too tight—the pieces should lie neatly together, without any puckering in the seam.

C. Proper alignment of shoulder seams

D. Sewing side and sleeve seams

SEWING THE SLEEVE TO THE BODY

Sewing the sleeves to the body is not as straight-forward as the other seams, as the pieces rarely line up in a stitch-to-stitch ratio. There are almost always more rows along the armhole section of the body than there are bound-off stitches along the top of the sleeve.

When sewing along the top of the sleeve, work just as you would for a shoulder seam, inserting the needle under the first stitch below the bind off. The armhole is sewn the same as the side seams, inserting the needle under the horizontal bar that runs between the selvedge stitch and the next stitch in (see photo A below).

The tricky part is figuring out how to ease the armhole into the top of the sleeve. Since the armhole has more rows than the sleeve top has stitches, you have to sew the armhole edge at a faster rate than you sew the sleeve.

Here is my standard formula for easing the armhole to the sleeve: *(Seam one stitch from the sleeve, then one stitch from the body) three times; then seam one stitch from the sleeve, two stitches from the body (meaning you insert your needle under two horizontal bars rather than just one). Repeat from * for the length of the seam, adjusting the seaming ratios further as needed.

I find that this formula works for most stocki-nette stitch sweaters. Sweaters knit in other stitch patterns may require a different seaming ratio, but this formula is still a good place to start.

A. Sewing the sleeve to the body

B. Three-needle bind off: insert the needle into the first stitches

THREE-NEEDLE BIND OFF (3 NDL BO)

Typically used to join shoulder seams, this technique seams and binds off two edges in one maneuver. The most common way to work a three-needle bind off is with the right sides of the pieces being sewn facing each other. This puts the ridge created by the technique on the inside of the garment. This is how you should work your three-needle bind offs, unless instructed otherwise.

Place the two pieces to be joined on two different needles. Hold the pieces parallel in your left hand.

Insert a third needle into the first stitch on the front needle, then into the first stitch on the back needle (see photo B on page 18), and knit these two stitches together (see photo C below).

*Knit the next two stitches together (two stitches on the right-hand needle), pass the first stitch on the right-hand needle over the second stitch and off the needle (see photo D below); repeat from * until all stitches are bound off.

A decorative element can be added by working with the wrong sides facing, which places the seam on the outside of the garment. This "outside seam" technique is used on the Striped Sweater (see page 71) to join the shoulder seams and join the sleeves to the body. When working a decorative three-needle bind off, it is important to note that there is a distinct front and back to the bind off. The side of the bind off facing you as you work is the knit side, and therefore fairly flat, while the side facing away from you is the nubbier purl side.

C. Three-needle bind off: knit stitches together

D. Three-needle bind off: pass the first stitch over the second stitch

If you want your shoulder bind offs to be identical, you have to work each of them in the same direction. This means work from the shoulder point to the neck on the first shoulder, then from the neck to the shoulder point on the second shoulder. If you do this with the front of the sweater facing you, the flat side will show on the sweater front; if you prefer to have the nubbier side at the sweater front, join the seams with the back of the sweater facing you.

BLOCKING

Blocking is just a fancy word for using steam or water to put the finishing touches on a knitted piece. Blocking smoothes out irregularities, tidies up seamed edges, and gives the garment its final shape.

To wet block, wash your project as instructed on the yarn label, then lay it out flat on towels and gently coax it into shape. You want to be careful here—you can stretch or distort your knitting by handling it roughly when it's wet.

Let your project dry completely, flipping it over a couple times and reshaping each time to the dimensions given in your pattern.

Lace, cables, and stranded (two-color patterned) projects usually require wet blocking to achieve their correct dimensions. For simpler patterns, steam blocking may be sufficient. To steam block, place your project on a covered surface (an ironing board for a small item, a table covered with towels for a larger item), turn your iron to a steam setting, and get your tape measure and pattern. Hold the steam iron an inch or so over your project and let the steam permeate the fabric. You never want to put the iron directly on your knitting, as doing so may scorch the fibers. Shape the piece to the size given in the pattern, then wait until the piece is completely cool and dry before moving it.

Be careful with acrylic and other man-made fibers, as steam heat may cause them to melt or otherwise alter in appearance. If you are unsure, use your swatch as a test piece before steaming your project.

Note on Knitting These Sweaters for Women

Although these designs were created for men, most can be worn by women as well. I do suggest shortening the sweater side seams by 1 to 2 inches. Women look best in sweaters that stop above the fullest part of their hips, and the lengths given in the patterns will run longer than that on most women (except those who are very tall).

ABBREVIATIONS

beg	beginning		psso	pass slipped stitch over
BO	bind off		ptbl	purl through back of the loop (see page 9)
CC	contrast color		pu	pick up (see page 16)
cn	cable needle		pwise	purlwise (see page 6)
CO	cast on (see page 7)		rem	remaining
dec	decrease (see page 11)		rep	repeat
dpn	double-pointed needle(s)		RS	right side (see page 6)
inc	increase (see page 10)		sk	skip
k	knit		sl	slip (see page 10)
k2tog	knit 2 together (see page 11)		sm	slip marker
kfb	knit front and back (see page 10)		ssk	slip slip knit (see page 12)
ktbl	knit through back of the loop (see page 9)		st(s)	stitch(es)
kwise	knitwise (see page 6)		St st	stockinette stitch (see page 6)
MC	main color		tog	together
p	purl		WS	wrong side (see page 7)
p2sso	pass 2 slipped stitches over		wyib	with yarn in back (see page 7)
p2tog	purl 2 together (see page 12)		wyif	with yarn in front (see page 7)
pm	place marker		YO	yarn over (see page 11)

Patterns

SEAWEED THROW

Rainy day. A good book. Stay warm. You're covered.

Undulating bands of knits and purls merge with mock cables in this luxurious throw. A bit of asymmetry adds visual interest, while the rib/welt patterning and double stranded yarn combine to create a dense, warm, and masculine design.

Size
$45^1/2$" x 53" [115.5 x 134.5 cm]

Materials
- 15 skeins ShibuiKnits Merino Kid (55% kid mohair, 45% merino wool; 216 yds [198 m] per 100 g skein) in Seaweed
- US size 10 [6 mm] circular needle, 32" [80 cm] or longer
- Tapestry needle
- Split ring markers (optional)

> It is useful to use markers between chart repeats to help you keep track of where you are. Because the chart shifts as you work, you need to use split ring markers, as these can be removed and replaced as you go.

Note
Yarn is worked double stranded (holding two strands together as one) throughout (see page 5).

Gauge
16 sts and 20 rows = 4" [10 cm] in St st with two strands of yarn held together

15 sts and 25 rows = approximately 4" [10 cm] in pattern with two strands of yarn held together

Pattern is elastic and gauge will vary slightly depending on how much it is stretched and where in the pattern you measure.

Special Techniques
Slip the first stitch of every row. If the first stitch of the row is knit, slip the stitch knitwise with the yarn in back. If the first stitch is purl, slip the stitch purlwise with the yarn in front.

CROSS 2 RIGHT
Knit the second stitch on the left-hand needle, then knit the first stitch.

This makes a "mini-cable," with the left stitch of the pair crossing over the right.

Seaweed Throw Chart

☐ Knit on RS, purl on WS   ☐ Purl on RS, knit on WS   ◼ Cross 2 right

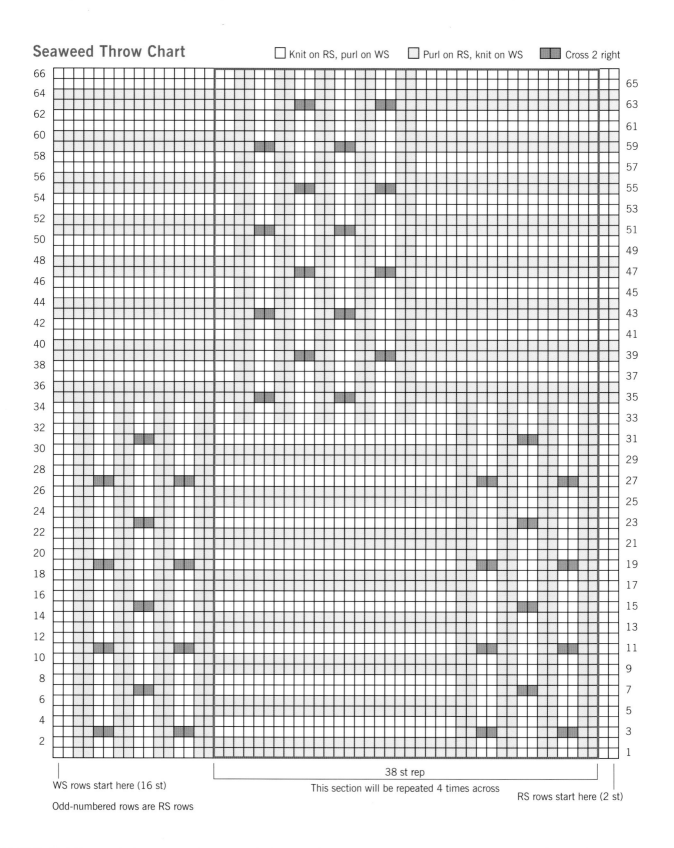

WS rows start here (16 st)

Odd-numbered rows are RS rows

38 st rep

This section will be repeated 4 times across

RS rows start here (2 st)

Directions

With two strands of yarn held together, CO 170 sts.

Work rows 1–66 of chart (see facing page)
5 times.

Next row: BO in pattern on row 1.

Finishing

Weave in ends. Throw should be only minimally blocked.

Merino Kid is a DK-weight yarn that is double stranded to get the above gauge. To substitute yarn, try double stranding a DK-weight yarn with similar fiber content. Another option is to use a heavy worsted-weight yarn that knits up at 4 sts per inch single stranded. Note that if you go with the single strand heavy worsted option, you will only need half the yardage listed.

SATURDAY MORNING SLIPPERS

Warm. Comfortable. Sit back and relax.

Knit with a double strand of worsted-weight yarn on a size 8 needle, these slippers are dense and warm. Knitting this tightly does slow things down, especially on the twisted garter stitch sole, but the end result is well worth the trouble. For the best fit, make a size that matches or is slightly larger than your foot circumference.

Sizes

S (M, L)

Finished foot circumference: 8 (9, 10)" [20 (23, 25.5) cm]

Finished foot length: 10 (10³/₄, 12)" [25.5 (27, 30.5) cm]

Materials

- Brown Sheep Company Lamb's Pride Worsted (85% wool, 15% mohair; 190 yds [174 m] per 113 g skein) in the following colors:

    For one-color version (shown at right on facing page):
    2 (3, 3) skeins M185 Aubergine

    For two-color version (shown at left on facing page):
    1 (2, 2) skeins M185 Aubergine
    1 (2, 2) skeins M89 Roasted Coffee

    (Another two-color version in M80 Blue Blood Red and M38 Lotus Pink is shown on page 31.)

- US size 8 [5 mm] circular needle, 24" [60 cm] long
- US size 8 [5 mm] double-pointed needles
- Waste yarn
- Stitch markers
- Tapestry needle

Note

Yarn is worked double stranded (holding two strands together as one) throughout (see page 5).

Gauge

16 sts and 24 rows = 4" [10 cm] in St st with two strands of yarn held together

18 sts and 32 rows = 4" [10 cm] in Twisted Garter Stitch with two strands of yarn held together

Special Techniques

TWISTED GARTER STITCH

Every row: Sl first st pwise wyib, then ktbl across row.

Directions

SOLE

This piece is knit side to side in Twisted Garter Stitch.

With circular needle and two strands of yarn, CO 39 (43, 46) sts. Do not join, but work back and forth in rows.

Increase rows:

Row 1: Sl first st pwise wyib, ktbl across.

Row 2: Sl first st pwise wyib, kfb, ktbl to last 3 sts, kfb, ktbl to end.

Repeat rows 1–2 a total of 3 (3, 4) times more— 47 (51, 56) sts.

Work 16 (20, 20) rows in Twisted Garter Stitch.

Decrease rows:

Row 1: Sl first st pwise wyib, ktbl, ssk, ktbl to last 3 sts, k2tog, ktbl to end.

Row 2: Sl first st pwise wyib, ktbl across.

Repeat rows 1–2 a total of 3 (3, 4) times more— 39 (43, 46) sts.

FOOT

Do not twist stitches in this section.

With circular needle, k39 (43, 46) sts, pm (first toe marker), pick up and k15 (17, 19) sts around toe, pm (second toe marker), pick up and k39 (43, 46) sts along cast-on edge, pm (first heel marker), pick up and k16 (18, 20) sts around heel, pm (second heel marker)—109 (121, 131) sts. This last marker also marks the start of your round.

> If you find you are one or two stitches short of the number of picked-up stitches along the cast-on edge, just increase to the correct number on the next round.

Rnd 1: K to 3 sts before first toe marker, ssk, k1, sm, k6 (7, 8), sl 2 tog kwise, k1, p2sso, k6 (7, 8), sm, k1, k2tog, k to 1 st past first heel marker, ssk, k to 3 sts before second heel marker, k2tog, k1.

Rnd 2 and all even rnds: K.

Rnd 3: K to 3 sts before first toe marker, ssk, k1, sm, k5 (6, 7), sl 2 tog kwise, k1, p2sso, k5 (6, 7), sm, k1, k2tog, k to 1 st past first heel marker, ssk, k to 3 sts before second heel marker, k2tog, k1.

Rnd 5: K to 3 sts before first toe marker, ssk, k1, sm, k4 (5, 6), sl 2 tog kwise, k1, p2sso, k4 (5, 6), sm, k1, k2tog, k to 1 st past first heel marker, ssk, k to 3 sts before second heel marker, k2tog, k1.

Rnd 7: K to 3 sts before first toe marker, ssk, k1, sm, k3 (4, 5), sl 2 tog kwise, k1, p2sso, k3 (4, 5), sm, k1, k2tog, k to 1 st past first heel marker, ssk, k to 3 sts before second heel marker, k2tog, k1.

Rnd 9: K to 3 sts before first toe marker, ssk, k1, sm, k2 (3, 4), sl 2 tog kwise, k1, p2sso, k2 (3, 4), sm, k1, k2tog, k to 1 st past first heel marker, ssk, k to 3 sts before second heel marker, k2tog, k1.

Rnd 11: K to 3 sts before first toe marker, ssk, k1, sm, k1 (2, 3), sl 2 tog kwise, k1, p2sso, k1 (2, 3), sm, k1, k2tog, k to 1 st past first heel marker, ssk, k to 3 sts before second heel marker, k2tog, k1.

Size S, skip to **.

Rnd 12: K.

Rnd 13: K to 3 sts before first toe marker, ssk, k1, sm, k— (1, 2), sl 2 tog kwise, k1, p2sso, k— (1, 2), sm, k1, k2tog, k to 1 st past first heel marker, ssk, k to 3 sts before second heel marker, k2tog, k1.

Size M, skip to **.

Rnd 14: K.

Rnd 15: K to 3 sts before first toe marker, ssk, k1, sm, k— (—, 1), sl 2 tog kwise, k1, p2sso, k— (—, 1), sm, k1, k2tog, k to 1 st past first heel marker, ssk, k to 3 sts before second heel marker, k2tog, k1.

Size L, continue to **.

**73 (79, 83) sts on needle.

Place first 17 (18, 19) sts of round on waste yarn; place next 18 (20, 21) sts on a dpn; place next 17 (19, 20) sts on a second dpn; place remaining 21 (22, 23) sts on waste yarn. Do not break yarn.

Remove markers as you work.

Using a separate, double strand of yarn, and working from the ankle toward the toe, graft the sts on the dpns together. One of the dpn will have 1 more st than the other, but this will not affect the look of the graft (see page 15)—just work until all sts have been joined.

CUFF

Place sts from waste yarn back onto dpn as follows: 17 (18, 19) sts on first dpn, 4 sts on second dpn (these are the 4 sts at the back of the heel), 17 (18, 19) sts on third dpn.

With the outside of the slipper facing you, and starting from the place where the yarn is still attached, k17 (18, 19) sts. You should be at the front of the ankle. Do not turn work.

Pick up and k2 sts along top of grafted seam, then k remaining 21 (22, 23) sts—40 (42, 44) sts. Place marker for beginning of rnd.

K 1 rnd.

Next rnd: K first 18 (19, 20) sts. Turn work.

You will work the rest of the cuff back and forth, to create the split at the front of the foot.

Work 5 rows in Twisted Garter Stitch. You can remove the beginning of round marker.

BO in knit. Do not twist sts on the bind-off row, as this will make the bind off too tight.

Weave in ends.

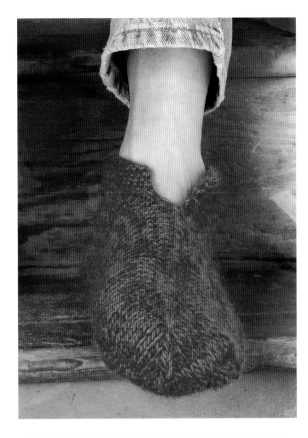

For tweedy, two-color slippers, use two tones of the same color yarn. This leaves you with a lot of leftover yarn, but you can use that for the Hiking Socks, a Top Down Hat, or the solid color version of the Nordic Hat.

BRITISH CHECKS SWEATER

Traditional patterning, modern construction.

Knit in the round up to the armholes, this sweater is then divided into the front and back sections and the remainder is worked flat. The sleeves are picked up from around the armhole and worked down to the cuff, eliminating sleeve seams and bulk in the underarm.

Sizes

S (M, L, XL)

Finished chest circumference: $40^1/2$ (44, 48, $51^1/2$)" [103 (112, 122, 131) cm]

Length: 25 (26, $27^1/4$, $28^3/4$)" [63.5 (66, 69, 73) cm]

Materials

- Rowan Felted Tweed (50% merino wool, 25% alpaca, 25% viscose; 175 yds [159 m] per 50 g skein) in the following colors:

    3 (4, 5, 5) skeins 145 Treacle (A)
    3 (4, 5, 5) skeins 156 Wheat (B)
    4 (5, 6, 6) skeins 150 Rage (C)

- US size 3 [3.25 mm] circular needle, between 24" and 32" [60 and 80 cm] long

- US size 3 [3.25 mm] circular needle, 16" [40 cm] long

- US size 3 [3.25 mm] double-pointed needles

- US size 4 [3.5 mm] circular needle, between 24" and 32" [60 and 80 cm] long

- US size 4 [3.5 mm] circular needle, 16" [40 cm] long

- US size 4 [3.5 mm] double-pointed needles

- US size 5 [3.75 mm] circular needle, between 24" and 32" [60 and 80 cm] long

- Stitch markers
- Stitch holder
- Tapestry needle

Gauge

26 sts and 34 rows = 4" [10 cm] in St st on size 4 [3.5 mm] needles

26 sts and 28 rows = 4" [10 cm] in chart pattern on size 5 [3.5 mm] needles

> Most people find their gauge changes when going from single color stockinette to a stranded color pattern, so it's important to swatch for both and adjust your needle sizes as necessary. See page 14 for more information on stranded color work.

Special Techniques

GARTER STITCH

Worked flat: Knit every row.

Worked in the round: Round 1: Purl. Round 2: Knit.

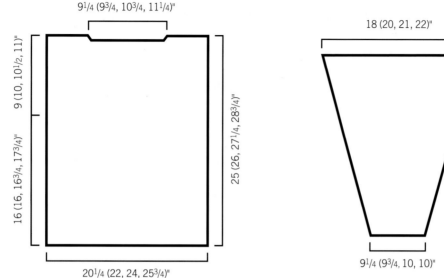

9¼ (9¾, 10¾, 11¼)"

9 (10, 10½, 11)"

16 (16, 16¾, 17¾)"

25 (26, 27¼, 28¾)"

20¼ (22, 24, 25¾)"

18 (20, 21, 22)"

18 (19, 20, 20½)"

9¼ (9¾, 10, 10)"

Directions

LOWER BODY

With the longer size 3 [3.25 mm] circular needle and A, CO 264 (288, 312, 336) sts. Join work into the round, being careful not to twist, and place marker.

Work in garter st for 6 rnds.

> It can be challenging to join this many stitches in the round without the stitches twisting over the needle. If you prefer, you can work the garter stitch portion flat, knitting every row for 6 rows, then join your work into the round. It's much easier to join without twisting once you have knit a few rows. You can use the tail from your cast on to sew up the little split at the side, and no one will be the wiser.

Change to size 5 [3.75 mm] circular needle and begin chart pattern (see facing page). Work through rnds 1–12 of chart 9 (9, 9, 10) times, then work through rnd 1 (1, 7, 1) one more time. Body measures about 16 (16, 16¾, 17¾)" [40.5 (40.5, 42, 45) cm] from cast on. (See page 12 for information on reading charts.)

DIVIDE FOR FRONT AND BACK

Work first 132 (144, 156, 168) sts following row 2 (2, 8, 2) of chart. Place remaining 132 (144, 156, 168) sts on holder (these will become the front sts).

Remainder of Back will be worked flat.

**Starting with row 3 (3, 9, 3), and working back and forth, work through row 12 of chart, slipping the first st of each row pwise and knitting the last st of each row with both A and B.

Sizes 40^1/$_2$, 44, and 51^1/$_2$" [103, 112, and 131 cm], work through row 1 (7, 7) one more time.

Size 48" [123 cm], work rows 1–12 one more time, then row 1 one more time.

All sizes: Break A and B.

Change to longer size 4 [3.5 mm] circular needle and C and work in St st until armhole measures 7^1/$_2$ (8^1/$_2$, 9, 9^1/$_2$)" [19 (21.5, 22.75, 24 cm)], ending with a WS row completed. (Do not slip the first st of the rows when working in C only.)

SHAPE NECK

K42 (46, 49, 53), join a second skein of C and BO center 48 (52, 58, 62) sts, k to end.

P 1 row.

Working both sides at the same time, dec 1 st at each side of neck on next and every following RS row 6 times as follows: K to 4 sts from neck edge, k2tog, k2; on second neck edge, k2, ssk, k to end—36 (40, 43, 47) sts on each side.

BO on next RS row.

FRONT

Place sts from holder back onto size 5 [3.75 mm] needle. Work as for back, starting from **, except begin chart at row 2 (2, 8, 2).

SLEEVES

Seam shoulders.

With size 4 [3.5 mm] 16" [40 cm] circular needle and C, starting at base of armhole, pick up and k118 (130, 136, 144) sts around armhole. Place marker for beginning of round.

K 8 rnds.

Dec on next rnd as follows: K2, k2tog, k to last 4 sts, ssk, k2. Repeat dec rnd on every following 5th rnd 28 (0, 0, 0) times; every 4th round 0 (28, 30, 23) times; every 2nd round 0 (4, 4, 15) times—60 (64, 66, 66) sts.

Switch to dpn when necessary.

British Checks Chart

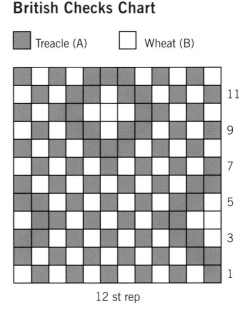

12 st rep

When working in the round, knit all stitches, and start each round at the right-hand side of the chart.

When working flat, knit on RS, purl on WS, and start at the right-hand side for RS rows, the left-hand side for WS rows.

Additionally, when working flat, slip the first stitch of the chart purlwise, and work the last stitch of the chart with both colors (knit on RS, purl on WS).

Work even until sleeve measures 18 (19, 20, 20^1/$_2$)" [45.5 (48.5, 51, 52) cm].

Change to size 3 [3.25 mm] dpn and work 5 rnds garter st. BO in k1, p1 rib.

FINISHING

With size 3 [3.25 mm] 16" [40 cm] circular needle and C, starting at right shoulder seam, pick up and k 10 sts along right back neck edge, 48 (52, 58, 62) sts along bound-off edge, 10 sts along left back neck edge, 10 sts along left front neck edge, 48 (52, 58, 62) sts along bound-off edge, 10 sts along right front neck edge—136 (144, 156, 164) sts. Place marker for beginning of round, and work 5 rnds garter st. BO in k1, p1 rib.

Weave in ends.

CLASSIC SOCKS

Detailed. Sophisticated. A keeper.

Finely knit with subtle pattern work on the leg, these elegant socks have a vintage feel. For a quicker-to-finish sock, omit the pattern and work the whole sock in stockinette. Or for a more colorful sock, use variegated yarn or multiple yarns to create stripes (see Options on page 40).

Sizes

S (M, L, XL)

Finished foot circumference: 7 (8, 9, 10)" [18 (20.5, 23, 25.5) cm]

Finished foot length: $8^{1}/4$ ($9^{1}/2$, $10^{1}/4$, $11^{1}/2$)" [21 (24, 26, 29) cm]

Materials

- ShibuiKnits Sock (100% superwash merino wool; 175 yds [159 m] per 50 g skein) in the following colors:

  For one-color version (shown on page 38):
  3 (3, 3, 4) skeins Sand

  For striped version (shown on page 40):
  2 (2, 2, 2) skeins Bark
  1 (1, 1, 1) skein Peacock
  1 (1, 1, 1) skein Sand

- Set of 5 US size 1 [2.25 mm] double-pointed needles

- Stitch markers

- Stitch holder

- Tapestry needle

Gauge

36 sts and 46 rounds = 4" [10 cm] in St st

36 sts and 53 rounds = 4" [10 cm] in Twisted Stitch Pattern

I get the same stitch gauge in stockinette as I do in the pattern stitch. However, you may not. It's a good idea to swatch for both, and adjust your needle size as necessary.

Special Techniques

TWISTED STITCH PATTERN

Worked in the round over a multiple of 9 sts.

Rnds 1 and 3: K.

Rnd 2: *K3, (k2tog leaving sts on left needle, k into the first st again, then drop both sts from left needle) 3 times, rep from * around.

Rnd 4: *K4, (k2tog leaving sts on left needle, knit into the first st again, then drop both sts from left needle) 2 times, k1, rep from * around.

Repeat these 4 rnds for Twisted Stitch Pattern.

If you are concerned about the cuff being tight on the calf, go ahead and knit the cuff on needles one size larger than those you use for the leg. When you finish the cuff, go back to the needles that give you the correct gauge.

You can also cast on and work just the first few rounds of the cuff on larger needles, then work the rest of the cuff and leg on the main needles. This is a good option if you tend to cast on tightly.

Directions

(If you are making the striped version, review the notes under Options on page 40 before you begin.)

CUFF

CO 62 (72, 80, 90) sts. Join into the round, placing marker at the beginning of the round.

Work in k1, p1 rib for 1$^{1}/_{2}$" [4 cm], inc 1 (0, 1, 0) st on last round—63 (72, 81, 90) sts.

LEG

Work in Twisted Stitch Pattern until leg measures 6 (7, 8, 9)" [15 (18, 20.5, 23) cm] from cast on, ending with rnd 4.

K 1 rnd.

HEEL

K17 (19, 21, 24) sts. Turn work and purl across 32 (36, 40, 46) sts. Place remaining 31 (36, 41, 44) sts on holder.

Work heel flap as follows:

Row 1: (Sl 1 pwise, k1) across.

Row 2: Sl first st pwise, p to end.

Repeat these 2 rows a total of 16 (18, 20, 23) times—32 (36, 40, 46) heel rows worked.

TURN HEEL

Row 1: K18 (20, 22, 25), k2tog tbl, k1, turn.

Row 2: Sl 1 pwise, p5, p2tog, p1.

Row 3: Sl 1 pwise, k6, k2tog tbl, k1.

Row 4: Sl 1 pwise, p7, p2tog, p1.

Row 5: Sl 1 pwise, k8, k2tog tbl, k1.

Row 6: Sl 1 pwise, p9, p2tog, p1.

Continue in this manner until all the heel sts have been worked, ending with a p2tog if there aren't enough sts for the final p1 on last row—18 (20, 22, 26) sts.

GUSSET

Knit across heel sts, keeping the heel sts on 1 needle. This will be needle #1.

With second dpn, pick up and k16 (18, 20, 23) sts along selvedge of heel flap. With third dpn, k31 (36, 41, 44) sts from holder. With fourth dpn, pick up and k16 (18, 20, 23) sts along second heel flap selvedge—81 (92, 103, 116) sts.

SHAPE GUSSET

Next rnd: K across needle #1. K to 3 sts before the end of needle #2, k2tog, k1. K across needle #3. On needle #4, k1, ssk, k to end of needle.

Next rnd: K.

Repeat these 2 rnds until 63 (72, 81, 90) sts remain.

Sizes 7" and 9" [18 and 23 cm] only: Dec as established at the end of needle #2 only one more time, k to end of rnd—62 (80) sts.

FOOT

Work even in St st until foot measures approximately 6$\frac{1}{2}$ (7$\frac{1}{2}$, 8, 9)" [16.5 (19, 20.5, 23) cm] from back of heel.

SHAPE TOE

Next rnd: K12 (15, 17, 19), k2tog, k2, ssk, k25 (30, 34, 39), k2tog, k2, ssk, k13 (15, 17, 20).

K 1 rnd.

Next rnd: K11 (14, 16, 18), k2tog, k2, ssk, k23 (28, 32, 37), k2tog, k2, ssk, k12 (14, 16, 19).

K 1 rnd.

Next rnd: K10 (13, 15, 17), k2tog, k2, ssk, k21 (26, 30, 35), k2tog, k2, ssk, k11 (13, 15, 18).

K 1 rnd.

Continue in this manner, working decs as established on every other rnd, until 30 (36, 40, 46) sts remain. Dec on every rnd until 14 (16, 16, 18) sts remain. Break yarn, leaving a 12" [30.5 cm] tail.

Divide sts between 2 needles: K the first 3 (4, 4, 4) sts of the next rnd, place next 7 (6, 6, 9) sts on another needle, place last 4 (4, 4, 5) sts on first needle—7 (8, 8, 9) sts per needle. Graft the toe stitches together (see page 15).

Weave in ends.

Options

If you prefer a plainer, non-patterned sock, follow the pattern as written, but knit all rounds after the ribbed cuff. As long as your stockinette gauge is the same as the pattern gauge, the socks will work either way.

The sock could be made in a solid color, a variegated yarn, or striped, as explained below.

Work cuff in Bark.

Work leg in St st, knitting each color for 3 rounds. Make the first stripe in the same color as the cuff to make the transition from the cuff to the St st smoother.

Knit leg until it is approximately the length given in the pattern, ending just before starting your next stripe in Bark.

Work heel flap and heel turn in Bark.

Pick up the stitches for the gusset with Bark. This counts as your first round of the next Bark stripe. You are resuming the stripe sequence with this round.

Work the rest of the gusset and foot as written, continuing your 3-round stripes. The color change should occur in the middle of needle #1 (at the bottom of the foot). Place a marker here to help you identify the start of the round.

Work the foot until it measures the length given in the pattern, ending with the third round of your current stripe color completed. Work the toe in Bark (working the toe in one of the other colors may require an additional skein of that color).

DAD'S SWEATER

Heirloom redux. Start your tradition, pass it on.

Inspired by a photo taken of my father (see page 45) as a young man in the 1960s wearing a sweater knit for him by one of his sisters, this is my version of a family classic. Without having the original sweater or pattern to work with, I interpreted the sweater based on the photograph alone. Rather than trying to recreate the yoke pattern precisely, I used it as a springboard to create my own design. I also changed the neckline (which appears to have a ribbed finish in the original) to a faced edge. I'd like to think my aunt would approve.

Sizes

S (M, L, XL)

Finished chest circumference: 40 (44$1/2$, 49, 53)" [106.5 (113, 124.5, 134.5) cm]

Length: 23$1/2$ (25, 26$3/4$, 27$1/2$)" [60 (63.5, 68, 70) cm]

Materials

- Rowan Scottish Tweed DK (100% wool; 123 yds [112 m] per 50 g skein) in the following colors:

    10 (12, 14, 16) skeins 31 Indigo (A)
    1 (1, 1, 1) skein 25 Oatmeal (B)

- US size 5 [3.75 mm] needles
- US size 7 [4.5 mm] needles
- US size 4 [3.5 mm] needles
- Stitch holder
- Tapestry needle

Gauge

22 sts and 28 rows = 4" [10 cm] in St st on size 5 [3.75 mm] needles

22 sts and 27 rows = 4" [10 cm] in chart pattern on size 7 [4.5 mm] needles

Special Techniques

SEED STITCH

All rows: K1, (p1, k1) to end.

> Most people find their gauge changes when going from single color stockinette to a stranded color pattern, so it's important to swatch for both and adjust your needle sizes as necessary. Using a size 5 and size 7 is what worked for me to get the correct gauge—you may find you need different sizes of needles to do the same. See page 14 for information on stranded color patterns.

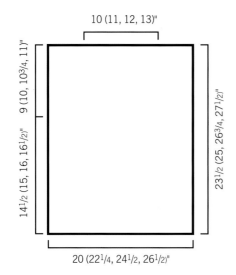

10 (11, 12, 13)"

9 (10, 10³/4, 11)"

14¹/2 (15, 16, 16¹/2)"

23¹/2 (25, 26³/4, 27¹/2)"

20 (22¹/4, 24¹/2, 26¹/2)"

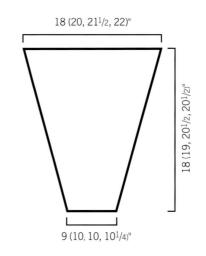

18 (20, 21¹/2, 22)"

18 (19, 20¹/2, 20¹/2)"

9 (10, 10, 10¹/4)"

Notes

The charted section of this sweater includes a selvedge stitch at the beginning and end of the row.

Work selvedge stitches as follows:

On RS rows: Sl the first st of the row pwise wyib, work chart across row to last st, k last st with both yarns.

On WS rows: Sl the first st of the row pwise wyif, work chart across row to last st, p last st with both yarns.

Working the selvedge stitches this way reduces the bulk at the side seam over the charted section and keeps the yarns in the correct position to work the pattern across the row.

Directions

BACK

With size 4 [3.5 mm] needles and A, CO 111 (123, 135, 147) sts.

Work Seed Stitch for 1¹/2" [4 cm].

Change to size 5 [3.75 mm] needles and work in St st until back measures 18³/4 (20¹/4, 22, 22³/4)"

[47.5 (51.5, 56, 58) cm] from cast on, ending with a WS row completed.

Change to size 7 [4.5 mm] needles and work rows 1–31 of chart. Row 31 will be a RS row.

(See page 12 for information on reading charts.)

(See note at beginning of pattern about working the selvedge sts over the charted section of the sweater.)

Change to size 5 [3.75 mm] needles and work 2 more rows in St st with A, ending with a RS row completed.

NECK FACING

Change to B and p 2 rows. This will create a purl ridge on the RS of the fabric.

Change to size 4 [3.5 mm] needles and A and work in St st for 1" [2.5 cm], starting with a WS (purl) row. BO.

FRONT

Work as for Back.

Dad's Sweater Chart

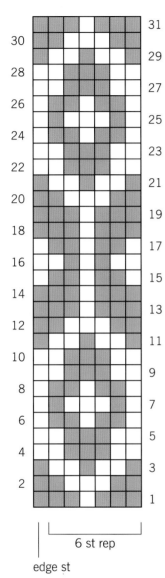

Rows are numbered on the sides: left side shows even numbers 2, 4, 6, 8, 10, 12, 14, 16, 18, 20, 22, 24, 26, 28, 30; right side shows odd numbers 1, 3, 5, 7, 9, 11, 13, 15, 17, 19, 21, 23, 25, 27, 29, 31.

■ Indigo (A)

□ Oatmeal (B)

Odd-numbered rows are RS rows.

The edge st is worked at the end of RS rows, and at the beginning of WS rows.

This chart does not include the selvege sts worked at the beginning and end of every row (see Notes on page 44).

6 st rep

edge st

SLEEVES

With size 4 [3.5 mm] needles and A, CO 51 (55, 55, 57) sts.

Work Seed Stitch for 1.5" [4 cm].

Change to size 5 [3.75 mm] needles and work in St st until sleeve measures 2" [5 cm] from cast on, ending with a WS row completed.

Inc 1 st at each end of next row and every following 4th row 19 (24, 31, 31) times more, then every 6th row 5 (3, 0, 0) times—101 (111, 119, 121) sts. Work even until sleeve measures 18 (19, 20^{1}/$_{2}$, 20^{1}/$_{2}$)" [45.5 (48, 52, 52) cm] from cast on. BO.

FINISHING

Tack neck facing into place.

Sew shoulder seams along purl ridge, sewing 5 (5^{1}/$_{2}$, 6^{1}/$_{4}$, 6^{3}/$_{4}$)" [12.5 (14, 16, 17) cm] for each shoulder.

Sew in sleeves. Sew sleeve and side seams.

Weave in ends.

ZIPPER CARDIGAN

Refined masculinity. Easy appeal.

Worked in one piece up to the armholes, this sweater features twisted stitches, mock cables, and a zipper closure—a contemporary alternative to the traditional buttoned-up cardigan. The zipper is sewn in by hand. With a little practice, you'll find that inserting zippers is so easy you may want to add them to all of your sweaters.

Sizes

S (M, L, XL)

Finished chest circumference: $40^1/2$ (44, $47^1/2$, 51)" [103 (112, 120.5, 129.5) cm]

Length: 23 (25, $25^1/2$, $25^1/2$)" [58.5 (63.5, 65, 65) cm]

Materials

- 9 (10, 11, 12) skeins ShibuiKnits Merino Alpaca (50% baby alpaca, 50% merino wool; 100 g, 132 yds [120 m] per 100 g skein) in Ivory.
- US size 8 [5 mm] circular needle, 24" [60 cm] or longer
- US size 7 [4.5 mm] circular needle, 24" [60 cm] or longer
- Waste yarn
- Tapestry needle
- 20 (22, 22, 22)" [51 (56, 56, 56) cm] separating zipper
- Sewing needle and thread that matches zipper color
- Stitch markers (optional)
- Row counter (optional)

Gauge

18 sts and 23 rows = 4" [10 cm] in Twisted Stockinette on size 8 [5 mm] needle

Special Techniques

TWISTED RIB

Row 1 (WS): P2, (k2 tbl, p2) to end.

Row 2 (RS): K2 tbl, (p2, k2 tbl) to end.

Repeat these 2 rows for Twisted Rib.

TWISTED STOCKINETTE

Row 1 (WS): P.

Row 2 (RS): K all sts tbl.

Repeat these 2 rows for Twisted Stockinette.

CABLE PATTERN

Worked over 6 sts.

Row 1 and all odd rows (WS): K2 tbl, p2, k2 tbl.

Row 2 (RS): P2, k2tog leaving these stitches on the left-hand needle, k into the first st again, drop the 2 sts from the left-hand needle, p2.

Rows 4 and 6: P2, k2 tbl, p2.

Repeat these 6 rows for Cable Pattern.

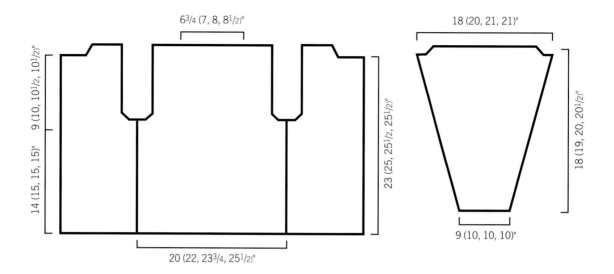

6³/₄ (7, 8, 8¹/₂)"

18 (20, 21, 21)"

9 (10, 10¹/₂, 10¹/₂)"

14 (15, 15, 15)"

23 (25, 25¹/₂, 25¹/₂)"

18 (19, 20, 20¹/₂)"

20 (22, 23³/₄, 25¹/₂)"

9 (10, 10, 10)"

TWISTED RIGHT-SLANTING DECREASE

Ktbl, insert right needle tip into next st on left needle as if to ptbl, slip it, and replace on the left-hand needle, so that the stitch is now twisted.

Transfer the ktbl just worked to the left needle, and pass the twisted st over it. Now transfer the ktbl back to the right-hand needle.

Directions

With size 8 [5 mm] needle, CO 182 (198, 214, 230) sts. Do not join, but work back and forth in rows. Work 5 rows in Twisted Rib.

Next row (RS): Work first 14 (14, 18, 18) sts in Twisted Stockinette, next 6 sts in Cable Pattern, next 142 (158, 166, 182) sts in Twisted Stockinette, next 6 sts in Cable Pattern, last 14 (14, 18, 18) sts in Twisted Stockinette. Because this is a RS row, you will be starting on row 2 of both patterns.

Work in Twisted Stockinette and Cable Pattern as set until you have completed 13 (14, 14, 14) repeats of the cable pattern. Sweater will measure

about 14 (15, 15, 15)" [35.5 (38, 38, 38) cm] from cast on. You should be ready to work a WS row.

Place stitch markers on either side of the cable panels if that helps you keep your place. Using a row counter takes the guess work out of tracking your cable rows.

DIVIDE FOR FRONTS AND BACK

Work 40 (44, 48, 52) sts, BO next 10 sts, work 82 (90, 98, 106) sts, BO next 10 sts, work last 40 (44, 48, 52) sts.

Place first 40 (44, 48, 52) sts and center 82 (90, 98, 106) sts on waste yarn. Turn work.

RIGHT FRONT

Continuing Twisted Stockinette and Cable Pattern as established, dec 1 st at armhole edge on next row as follows: Work to last 4 sts, work a Twisted Right-Slanting Decrease, work to end of row. Dec as established on every following RS row 7 (8, 9, 11) times more—32 (35, 38, 40) sts.

Work even until you have completed a total of 16 (17, 18, 18) repeats of Cable Pattern. From this point forward, omit Cable Pattern and work in Twisted Stockinette only until Right Front measures 20 (22, 22, 22)" [58.5 (63.5, 65, 65) cm] from cast on, ending with a WS row.

SHAPE NECK

BO 7 (9, 9, 10) sts at beginning of next row— 25 (26, 29, 30) sts.

Next row (WS): Dec 1 st at neck edge as follows: Work to last 4 sts, p2tog tbl, work to end of row. Dec as established on every following WS row 6 (6, 8, 8) times more—18 (19, 20, 21) sts. Work even until Right Front measures 23 (25, 25^1/$_2$, 25^1/$_2$)" [58.5 (63.5, 65, 65) cm]. BO.

LEFT FRONT

With RS facing, place 40 (44, 48, 52) sts from waste yarn back onto needle. Join yarn at armhole edge and work 1 row.

Next row (WS): Dec 1 st at armhole edge this row as follows: Work to last 4 sts, p2tog tbl, work to end of row. Dec as established on every following WS row 7 (8, 9, 11) times more—32 (35, 38, 40) sts.

Work even until you have completed a total of 16 (17, 18, 18) repeats of Cable Pattern. From this point forward, omit Cable Pattern and work in Twisted Stockinette only until Left Front measures 20 (22, 22, 22)" [58.5 (63.5, 65, 65) cm] from cast on, ending with a RS row completed.

SHAPE NECK

BO 7 (9, 9, 10) sts at beginning of next row.

Next row (RS): Dec 1 st at neck edge as follows: Work to last 4 sts, work a Twisted Right-Slanting Decrease, work to end of row. Dec as established on every following RS row 6 (6, 8, 8) times more—18 (19, 20, 21) sts. Work even in pattern until Left Front measures 23 (25, 25^1/$_2$, 25^1/$_2$)" [58.5 (63.5, 65, 65) cm]. BO.

BACK

With RS facing, place 82 (90, 98, 106) sts from waste yarn back onto needle. Join yarn and continue in Twisted Stockinette. Dec at armholes as follows:

Row 1 (RS): Work to last 4 sts, work a Twisted Right-Slanting Decrease, work to end of row.

Row 2 (WS): Work to last 4 sts, p2tog tbl, work to end of row.

Repeat rows 1 and 2 a total of 7 (8, 9, 11) times more—66 (72, 78, 82) sts.

Work even until Back measures 23 (25, 25^1/$_2$, 25^1/$_2$)" [58.5 (63.5, 65, 65) cm] from cast on. BO.

SLEEVES

With size 8 [5 mm] needle, CO 42 (46, 46, 46) sts. Do not join, but work back and forth in rows. Work 5 rows in Twisted Rib.

Work in Twisted Stockinette, starting with row 2 (RS) until sleeve measures 1^1/$_2$" [4 cm] from cast on, ending with a WS row.

Inc 1 st at each end of next row and every following 4th row 10 (13, 19, 18) times more, then every following 6th row 9 (8, 5, 6) times—82 (90, 96, 96) sts.

> When working the sleeve increases, just do your usual increase. Trying to twist the increase will only make your life difficult.

Work even until sleeve measures 18 (19, 20, 20$\frac{1}{2}$)" [45.5 (48, 51, 52) cm] from cast on, ending with a WS row completed.

BO 5 sts at beginning of next 2 rows—72 (80, 86, 86) sts.

Shape sleeve cap as follows:

Row 1 (RS): Work to last 4 sts, work a Twisted Right-Slanting Decrease, work to end of row.

Row 2 (WS): Work to last 4 sts, p2tog tbl, work to end of row.

Repeat rows 1 and 2 a total of 7 (8, 9, 11) times more—56 (62, 66, 62) sts. BO.

FINISHING

Sew shoulder seams.

Sew sleeves into place.

Sew sleeve seams.

FRONT BANDS

With size 7 [4.5 mm] circular needle, pick up and k90 (100, 100, 100) sts along right front. K 3 rows, knitting all sts tbl.

Next row (RS): BO in purl.

Repeat on the left front.

INSERT ZIPPER

With RS facing and zipper closed, pin zipper into place, so that the zipper teeth are just covered by the front edges of the fabric. Working from RS, with matching sewing thread and needle, stitch the zipper to the fabric, working close to the fabric edge and keeping your stitches short on the outside of the fabric (they should disappear into the knitting).

Unzip zipper, turn work inside out, and sew edge of zipper tape to the fabric.

NECK BAND

With size 7 [4.5 mm] circular needle, pick up and k22 (24, 27, 28) sts along right front neck, 30 (32, 36, 38) sts along back neck, 22 (24, 27, 28) sts along left front neck—74 (80, 90, 94) sts.

K 3 rows, knitting all sts tbl.

Next row (RS): BO in purl.

Weave in ends.

NORDIC HAT—THREE WAYS

Three styles. Bold stars, dancing ladies, or classic simplicity.

Here is a basic knit hat, with multiple options. Make it with or without earflaps, with dancing figures, or with a bold Nordic star. The earflap ties can be simple I-cord or the more colorful and unusual braided cord. The simplest version of the hat knits up in less than a day; the more fanciful versions don't take much longer (see Options on page 54).

Once you get the basic pattern down, feel free to interpret it as you like, adding your own unique motifs and embellishments.

Size
Finished circumference: 21^1/$_2$" [54.5 cm]

Materials
- Brown Sheep Company Lamb's Pride Worsted (85% wool, 15% mohair; 190 yds [174 m] per 113 g skein) in the following colors (see box at right):
  - 1 skein M140 Aran (A)
  - 1 skein M80 Blue Blood Red (B)
  - 1 skein M113 Oregano (C)
- US size 7 [4.5 mm] double-pointed needles
- US size 7 [4.5 mm] circular needle, 16" [40 cm] long
- Stitch marker
- Tapestry needle

Gauge
20 sts and 28 rounds = 4" [10 cm] in St st

The given quantity of yarn will allow you to make all three versions of the hat shown, if you use a different color as the main color for each version.

For the Dancing Granny Hat, Aran is the main color.

For the Star Hat, Blue Blood Red is the main color.

For the plain hat, Oregano is the main color.

Special Techniques
DOT STITCH

Rnds 1 and 3: K.

Rnd 2: (P1, k1) around.

Rnd 4: (K1, p1) around.

Repeat these 4 rnds for Dot Stitch.

Directions

EARFLAPS

For earflaps with I-cord ties:

Using main color and dpn, CO 3 sts and work in I-cord (see page 15) until tie measures about 13" [33 cm], or desired length.

Begin earflap:

Row 1 (RS): Kfb twice, k1—5 sts.

Row 2 and all WS rows: K1, (p1, k1) to end.

Row 3: Kfb, k to last 2 sts, kfb, k1—7 sts.

Repeat rows 2 and 3 until you have 25 sts on the needle, ending with a WS row completed. Break yarn and leave on dpn. Make second earflap in same manner as first. Go to "Cast on for hat."

For earflaps with braided cord ties:

With main color, CO 3 sts and begin earflap immediately (omitting I-cord step). Work as given above until you have 25 earflap sts, ending with a WS row completed. Go to "Cast on for hat."

See end of pattern for how to make and attach braided cords.

> The irregularity of the Star motif may cause you to knit looser than if you were knitting the more regular Dancing Granny chart or the plain stockinette version of the hat. It's hard to get a rhythm going when working this motif, so the knitting tends to be more relaxed. The star hat will still fit most adults; it just may be a bit taller and looser.

Cast on for hat:

Using circular needle and main color, CO 108 sts. Join for working in the round, being careful not to twist, and place marker at beginning of round.

Join earflaps to hat:

Working in Dot Stitch pattern beginning with rnd 1, work 14 sts. Holding earflap behind hat sts (both sets of sts in your left hand, with needles parallel and right sides of both earflap and hat facing you), join earflap to hat by knitting the first earflap st together with the next hat st, then *k the next earflap st together with the next hat st, rep from * until all earflap sts have been worked. Work across next 30 hat sts, join second earflap in the same manner as the first, work remaining 15 sts.

Continue in Dot Stitch until you have worked through rnds 1–4 a total of 2 times. K 2 rnds. Begin either Dancing Granny chart (see page 56) or Star chart (see page 57). After completing chart, k 1 rnd in main color.

Crown decreases:

Change to dpn when there are too few sts to work on circular needle.

Next rnd: (K10, k2tog) around—99 sts.

Next rnd: K.

Next rnd: (K9, k2tog) around—90 sts.

Next rnd: K.

Next rnd: (K8, k2tog) around—81 sts.

Next rnd: K.

Continue in this manner, alternating a dec rnd with a plain k rnd and working 1 fewer st between decs on every dec rnd, until you have completed the (k1, k2tog) rnd—18 sts.

Last rnd: K2tog around—9 sts.

Break yarn leaving an 8" [20.5 cm] tail. Thread yarn through tapestry needle and draw through remaining sts. Fasten off.

Options

For a flapless hat, CO 108 sts with main color, work Dot Stitch for 8 rounds, and proceed with hat as written.

For a stockinette hat, follow pattern as written, with or without earflaps, eliminating charts. Instead, after completing Dot Stitch border, k30 rnds (about $4^1/2$" [11.5 cm]), then proceed with crown shaping as written.

This makes a great basic hat, and it's a good foundation for embroidery or other embellishment, if you like that sort of thing.

TO MAKE BRAIDED CORD

Round braids have several advantages over I-cords. They are stronger and less prone to stretching, you can make them with multiple colors, and, in my opinion, they are more fun to make.

This is a 4-strand round braiding technique. Each strand is composed of two lengths of a single color held together to make one strand.

I made my cord with three colors.

To make cord as shown:

Cut 2, 40" [102 cm] lengths each Blue Blood Red and Oregano.

Cut 4, 40" [102 cm] lengths Aran.

This makes 1 strand Blue Blood Red, 1 strand Oregano, and 2 strands Aran (remember that each strand is composed of two lengths held together as one).

Tie the strands to a chair back, drawer pull, etc. You need to tie them to something that will be stable as you pull on the strands. If you tie them around something with a circumference of more than a couple inches, you may want to cut your lengths a bit longer, to compensate for the length you will lose in tying.

I tied my strands in the following order (from left to right): Aran, Blue Blood Red, Aran, Oregano. This will make the colors spiral around the cord. If you tie the strands in Aran, Aran, Blue Blood Red, Oregano, you will have straight lines of color running the length of the cord. Either version is attractive. Experiment to see what you like best.

Going from left to right, number each strand: the first Aran strand is #1, the Blue Blood Red strand is #2, the second Aran strand is #3, the Oregano strand is #4.

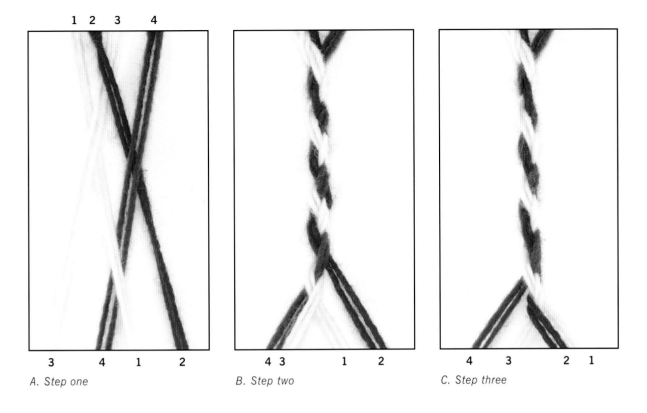

1 2 3   4

3   4   1   2

A. Step one

4 3   1   2

B. Step two

4   3   2   1

C. Step three

To work the braid:

1. Bring strand #2 over strand #3 and under strand #4. Then bring strand #1 under strand #3 and over strand #4. The strands are now in the following order: #3 is on the far left, #4 and #1 are in the center, and #2 is at the far right (see photo A above).

2. Take strand #3 (which is now the outside left strand) under the center two strands, then up between strands #1 and #2, finally crossing over strand #1. Strands are now in the following order: #4 is on the far left, #3 and #1 are in the center, and #2 is on the far right (see photo B above).

3. Take strand #2 (outside right strand) under the center two strands, up between strands #4 and #3, finally crossing over strand #3. Strands are now in the following order: #4 is on the far left, #3 and #2 are in the center, and #1 is on the far right (see photo C above).

You can see that the positions of the strands are constantly changing. So you want to get to the point where you don't have to think about what number strand is where, and instead work from an understanding of the braiding sequence.

Simplified braiding sequence:

1. Bring strand #2 over strand #3 and under strand #4. Then bring strand #1 under strand #3 and over strand #4.

2. Take the outside left strand under the center two strands, then up between the two far right strands, finally crossing over the second strand from the right.

3. Take the outside right strand under the center two strands, up between the two far left strands, finally crossing over the second strand in from the left.

4. Repeat steps 1–3 until braid is desired length.

When your braid is long enough, tie a knot at the lower end, about ¹/₂" [1 cm] from the end of the braid. Cut the yarn 1" [2.5 cm] or so from the base of the knot.

Tie another knot at the top of the braid, then cut the yarn free from the chair back or whatever you had it tied to. Trim the yarn ends so they are even.

You can sew the braid to the earflaps any way that appeals to you. I like to fold the braid back on itself about 5" [12.5 cm], then sew the fold to the inside of the earflap, about ¹/₂" [1 cm] from the tip. Use your knitting yarn to sew, and do sew all the way around the braid, so it is very securely attached to the hat.

Dancing Granny Chart

Knit all stitches in color shown.

 Aran (A)

 Blue Blood Red (B)

Oregano (C)

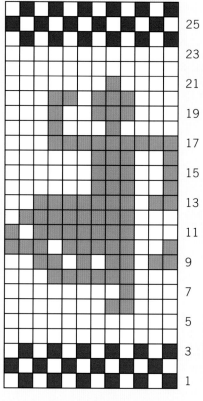

12 st rep

Star Chart

Knit all stitches in color shown.

☐ Aran (A)   ■ Blue Blood Red (B)

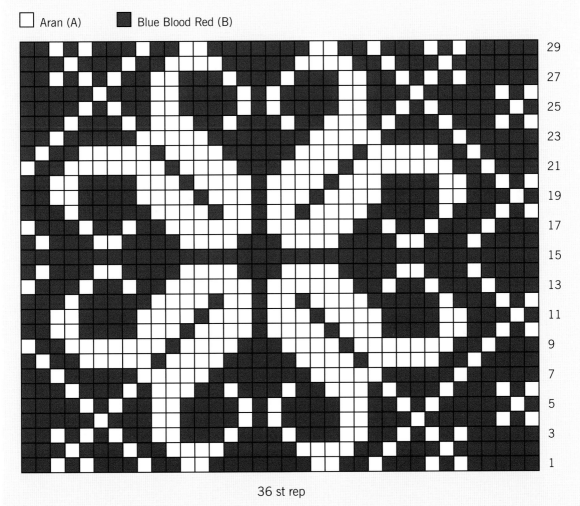

36 st rep

NO FRILLS MITTENS

Rustic. Multipurpose. The best-fit mitt you'll find.

This is a basic mitten with a really great fit—snug to the hand but not too tight. Because it is so simple, you can easily add cables, embroidery, or other embellishments to the basic design. I have given an option for a fingerless version, using a technique for making stripes out of a single color of variegated yarn (see Fingerless Version on page 61).

Sizes

S (M, L)

Finished hand circumference: $7^1/4$ (8, $8^3/4$)" [18.5 (20.5, 22) cm]

Materials

- Brown Sheep Company Lamb's Pride Worsted (85% wool, 15% mohair; 190 yds [174 m] per 113 g skein) in the following colors:

    For one-color version:
    1 skein M06 Deep Charcoal

    (Another one-color version in M83 Raspberry is shown on page 106.)

    For fingerless version (shown on page 61):
    1 (2, 2) skeins Noro Kureyon (100% wool; 109 yds [100 m] per 50 g skein) in color #149
- US size 5 [3.75 mm] double-pointed needles
- US size 7 [4.5 mm] double-pointed needles
- Stitch markers
- Waste yarn

Gauge

20 sts and 26 rounds = 4" [10 cm] in St st on size 7 [4.5 mm] needles

Special Techniques

BORDER PATTERN

Rnds 1 and 3: K.

Rnd 2: (P1, k1) around.

Round 4: (K1, p1) around.

Repeat rnds 1–4 for Border Pattern.

Directions

(If you are making the fingerless version, review the notes on page 61 before you begin.)

CUFF

With size 5 [3.75 mm] dpn, CO 36 (40, 44) sts. Join into the round, placing marker at the beginning of the round. Begin Border Pattern. Work through Border Pattern 4 times.

K 3 rounds.

For mittens that really keep the rain and snow off your wrist, work through the border pattern a few more times—8 repeats makes for a good, deep cuff.

HAND AND THUMB GUSSET

Change to size 7 [4.5 mm] dpn and shape thumb gusset as follows:

Next rnd: Kfb, k1, kfb, k to end of rnd.

K 1 rnd.

Next rnd: Kfb, k3, kfb, k to end.

K 2 rnds.

Next rnd: Kfb, k5, kfb, k to end.

K 1 rnd.

Next rnd: Kfb, k7, kfb, k to end.

K 2 rnds.

Next rnd: Kfb, k9, kfb, k to end. For small, go to **.

K1 rnd.

Next rnd: Kfb, k11, kfb, k to end. For medium, go to **.

K 2 rnds.

Next rnd: Kfb, k13, kfb, k to end. For large, go to **.

**Next rnd: K1, place next 12 (14, 16) sts on waste yarn (these will become the thumb), CO 2 sts with the backward loop method (see page 9), k to end of rnd.

Work even in St st on remaining 36 (40, 44) hand sts until mitten measures $5^{1}/4$ ($5^{3}/4$, $6^{1}/4$)" [13.5 (14.5, 16) cm] from top of cuff, or until mitten reaches the tip of the little finger when tried on.

SHAPE TOP

Next rnd: *K7 (8, 9), k2tog; rep from * around.

Next rnd: K.

Next rnd: *K6 (7, 8), k2tog; rep from * around.

Next rnd: K.

Next rnd: *K5 (6, 7), k2tog; rep from * around.

Next rnd: K.

Next rnd: *K4 (5, 6), k2tog; rep from * around.

Next rnd: K.

Continue in this manner, alternating a dec rnd with a plain k rnd and working 1 fewer st between decs with each subsequent dec rnd, until you have completed the k1, k2tog rnd—8 sts.

Graft these sts together (see page 15), or gather by threading tail of yarn through sts and drawing closed.

THUMB

Place 12 (14, 16) thumb sts from waste yarn back onto dpn. Join yarn and k12 (14, 16) thumb sts, then pick up and k3 sts from where sts were CO above thumb—15 (17, 19) sts.

Next rnd: K to last 2 sts, k2tog—14 (16, 18) sts.

Work even in St st until thumb measures $1^{3}/4$ (2, $2^{1}/2$)" [4.5 (5, 6.5) cm] from where sts were picked up.

Small:

*K1, k2tog, k2, k2tog; rep from * around—10 sts.

K 1 rnd.

*K2tog, k1, k2tog; rep from * once more—6 sts.

Break yarn and graft or gather sts tog.

*K2, k2tog; rep from * around—12 sts.

K 1 rnd.

K2tog around—6 sts.

Break yarn and graft or gather sts tog.

*K1, k2tog; rep from * around—12 sts.

K 1 rnd.

K2tog around—6 sts.

Break yarn and graft or gather sts tog.

FINGERLESS VERSION

Use the striping technique described in the Top Down Hats pattern (see page 115).

Work as for regular mitten until mitten measures 3 ($3^1/2$, 4)" [7.5 (9, 10) cm] from top of cuff, or $1/2$" [1 cm] less than desired length.

With size 5 [3.75 mm] needles, work in Border Pattern for 5 rnds. BO in pattern on rnd 6.

Work thumb as for regular mitten, until thumb measures $3/4$ (1, $1^1/2$)" [2 (2.5, 4) cm] from picked up sts, or $1/2$" [1 cm] less than desired length.

With size 5 [3.75 mm] needles, work in Border Pattern for 3 rnds. BO in pattern on rnd 4.

HIKING SOCKS

The outdoors are calling. Pull up your socks and answer.

Inspired by old photos of rugged socks that had been repaired at the heels and toes with contrast color yarn, these socks knit up quickly and are a good way to use up small amounts of yarn left over from other projects. The twisted rib has a tidier look than standard rib, and holds its shape better as well.

Sizes

S (M, L)

Finished foot circumference: $7^1/_4$ ($8^1/_2$, $9^1/_2$)" [18.5 (21.5, 24) cm]

Finished foot length: $8^1/_2$ (10, 11)" [21.5 (25.5, 28) cm]

Materials

- Brown Sheep Company Lamb's Pride Worsted (85% wool, 15% mohair; 190 yds [174 m] per 113 g skein) in the following colors:

    For tall socks (shown at left on feet):
    1 (2, 2) skeins M01 Sandy Heather (B)

    Small amounts M83 Raspberry (A), M38 Lotus Pink (C), and M06 Deep Charcoal (D)

    For regular socks (shown at left over boots):
    1 (2, 2) skeins M115 Oatmeal (B)

    Small amounts M185 Aubergine (A), M06 Deep Charcoal (C), and M02 Brown Heather (D)

- US size 7 [4.5 mm] double-pointed needles
- Stitch markers
- Stitch holder
- Tapestry needle

Gauge

20 sts and 26 rounds = 4" [10 cm] in St st

Special Techniques

RIB PATTERN

Rnd 1: (K2, p1) around.

Rnd 2: (K2 tbl, p1) around.

Repeat these 2 rnds for Rib Pattern.

> If you need socks a bit larger than the last size given here, knitting the sock as written for the largest size, but on size 8 [5 mm] needles, should do the trick. Just add about $^1/_2$" [1 cm] to the length of the foot before shaping the toe.

Directions

With A and size 7 [4.5 mm] dpn, CO 36 (42, 48) sts. Join for working in the round, placing marker at the beginning of the round.

Work in Rib Pattern for $2^1/_2$" [6.5 cm], ending with rnd 2 completed. Break A.

Join B and k 1 rnd.

Continue in Rib Pattern, starting with rnd 2, until sock measures 8 (8, 9)" [20.5 (20.5, 23) cm] from cast on, ending with rnd 2 completed. Break B.

> For tall socks, keep knitting in main color until sock is desired length; 12–14" [30.5–35.5 cm] from cast on is good for a sock that will reach to just below the knee. For larger calves, consider knitting the first few inches of the sock on a size 8 [5 mm] needle.

HEEL

Place the first 9 (10, 12) sts and the last 9 (10, 12) sts of the round onto 1 dpn. Place the remaining 18 (22, 24) sts on a stitch holder.

Join C. With WS facing, p across 18 (20, 24) heel sts.

Work heel flap as follows:

Row 1: (Sl 1 pwise, k1) across.

Row 2: Sl first st pwise, p to end.

Repeat these 2 rows 8 (9, 11) times more—18 (20, 24) heel rows worked.

TURN HEEL

Row 1: K11 (12, 14), k2tog, k1, turn.

Row 2: Sl 1 pwise, p5, p2tog, p1.

Row 3: Sl 1 pwise, k6, k2tog, k1.

Row 4: Sl 1 pwise, p7, p2tog, p1.

Continue in this manner until all heel sts have been worked, ending with a p row—12 (12, 14) heel sts. Break C.

GUSSET

Sl first 6 (6, 7) heel sts onto a second dpn. Join B and k next 6 (6, 7) heel sts (your yarn will be joined in the middle of the 12 [12, 14] heel sts, which is the new beginning of the round).

Pick up and k9 (10, 12) sts along side of heel flap, place marker (this will be a "gusset marker"), k18 (22, 24) sts from holder, place marker (another "gusset marker"), pick up and k9 (10, 12) sts along other side of heel flap, k6 (6, 7) remaining heel sts—48 (54, 62) sts.

SHAPE GUSSET

Next round: K to 2 sts before first gusset marker, k2tog. K to next gusset marker, sm, ssk. K to end of rnd.

Next round: K.

Repeat these 2 rnds until 36 (42, 48) sts remain.

FOOT

Work even in St st until foot measures approximately 6$\frac{1}{2}$ (8, 8$\frac{1}{2}$)" [16.5 (20.5, 21.5) cm] from back of heel. Break B. Join D and k 1 rnd.

SHAPE TOE

Next rnd: K6 (7, 9), k2tog, k2, ssk, k12 (15, 18), k2tog, k2, ssk, k6 (8, 9).

Next rnd: K.

Next rnd: K5 (6, 8), k2tog, k2, ssk, k10 (13, 16), k2tog, k2, ssk, k5 (7, 8).

Next rnd: K.

Continue in this manner, decreasing as established on every other rnd, with 1 fewer st between decs on each successive rnd, until 16 (26, 24) sts remain. Dec as established on every rnd until 12 (14, 12) sts remain. Break yarn, leaving a 12" [30.5 cm] tail. Divide remaining sts between 2 needles: k the first 3 (3, 3) sts of the next rnd, place next 6 (7, 6) sts on another needle, place last 3 (4, 3) sts on first needle—6 (7, 6) sts per needle. Graft the toe stitches together (see page 15).

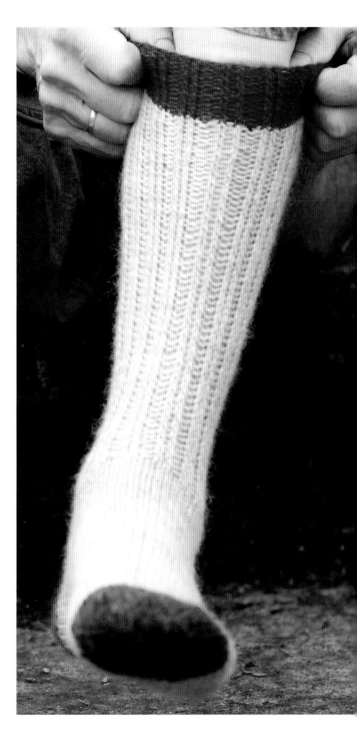

EVERYDAY SWEATER

The go-to sweater. The no-brainer. Put it on and get going.

My version of the everyday, simple sweater offers a few tweaks. Twisted ribs at the cuffs and hems, a bold intarsia color block at the back. I also used a yarn with subtle color variation, adding depth to the stockinette stitch fabric. These elements come together to create a sweater that can become a staple in any man's wardrobe. Use the yarn left over from the colorblock to make Top Down Hats (see page 115).

Sizes

S (M, L, XL)

Finished chest circumference: 40^1/$_2$ (44, 48, 51^1/$_2$)" [103 (112, 122, 131) cm]

Length: 23^1/$_2$ (25, 26^1/$_2$, 27)" [59.5 (63.5, 67.5, 68.5) cm]

Materials

- ShibuiKnits Merino Kid (55% kid mohair, 45% merino wool; 216 yds [197 m] per 100 g skein) in the following colors:

    6 (7, 8, 9) skeins Bark (A)
    1 (1, 1, 1) skein Wasabi (B)

- US size 6 [4 mm] needles
- US size 6 [4 mm] circular needle, 16" [40 cm] long
- US size 6 [4 mm] double-pointed needles (optional)
- Stitch markers
- Tapestry needle
- Stitch holder

Gauge

22 sts and 29 rows = 4" [10 cm] in St st

Special Techniques

TWISTED RIB

Worked flat:

Row 1 (WS): P2, (k3 tbl, p2) to end.

Row 2 (RS): K2 tbl, (p3, k2 tbl) to end.

Repeat these 2 rows for Twisted Rib.

Worked in the round:

Rnd 1: (K2 tbl, p3) around.

Rnd 2: (K2, p3) around.

Repeat these 2 rnds for Twisted Rib.

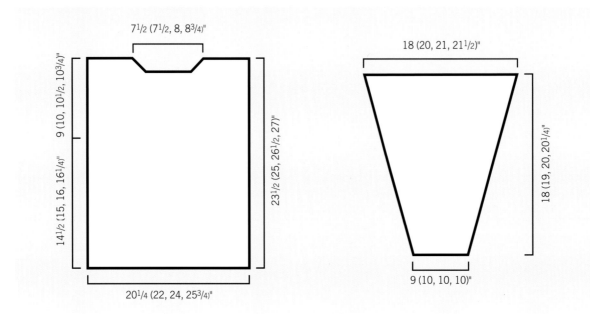

7¹/₂ (7¹/₂, 8, 8³/₄)"

9 (10, 10¹/₂, 10³/₄)"

14¹/₂ (15, 16, 16¹/₄)"

23¹/₂ (25, 26¹/₂, 27)"

20¹/₄ (22, 24, 25³/₄)"

18 (20, 21, 21¹/₂)"

18 (19, 20, 20¹/₄)"

9 (10, 10, 10)"

Directions

FRONT

With size 6 [4 mm] needle and A, CO 112 (122, 132, 142) sts.

Work 10 rows in Twisted Rib.

Starting with a p (WS) row, work in St st until front measures 20¹/₂ (22, 23¹/₂, 24)" [52 (56, 59.5, 61) cm] from cast on, ending with a WS row completed.

SHAPE NECK

K46 (51, 55, 58), join new skein and k20 (20, 22, 26), then place these 20 (20, 22, 26) sts on holder.

K remaining 46 (51, 55, 58) sts.

Working both sides at once, BO 2 sts at each neck edge 3 times—40 (45, 49, 52) sts each side.

Next RS row: K to 4 sts from neck edge, k2tog, k2; on second neck edge, k2, ssk, k to end.

Work decs as established on every following RS row 4 times more—35 (40, 44, 47) sts each side.

Work even until Front measures 23¹/₂ (25, 26¹/₂, 27)" [59.5 (63.5, 67.5, 68.5) cm] from cast on. BO.

BACK

Work as for Front until Back measures 16¹/₂ (17¹/₂, 18¹/₂, 19)" [42 (44.5, 47, 48.5) cm] from cast on, ending with a WS row completed.

Next row: K48 (53, 58, 63) with A, k16 with B, k48 (53, 58, 63) with A. See page 15 for information on intarsia knitting.

Next row: P48 (53, 58, 63) with A, p16 with B, p48 (53, 58, 63) with A.

Rep these 2 rows 10 times more, then work first row once more—23 colorblock rows worked. Break B.

Continue in St st with A only until Back measures same as Front to shoulders, ending with a WS row completed. BO.

SLEEVES

Seam shoulders.

Place markers 9 (10, 10^1/$_2$, 10^3/$_4$)" [23 (25.5, 26.5, 27) cm] on either side of shoulder seam.

With RS facing, using circular needle and A, pick up and k100 (111, 115, 119) sts between markers.

Join in the round, placing marker at start of round.

K 8 (8, 8, 6) rnds.

Dec on next rnd as follows: K2, k2tog, k to last 4 sts, ssk, k2. Dec as established on every following 6th rnd 4 (2, 3, 0) times more, then every 4th rnd 20 (25, 26, 31) times—50 (55, 55, 55) sts. Change to dpn when necessary.

Work even until sleeve measures 16^1/$_2$ (17^1/$_2$, 18^1/$_2$, 18^1/$_2$)" [42 (44.5, 47, 47) cm].

Work 9 rnds in Twisted Rib. BO in pattern.

> You may find that you can knit the whole sleeve on a 16" [40 cm] circular needle. But if the knitting gets awkward as you move toward the cuff, switch to double-pointed needles.

NECKBAND

With RS facing, using circular needle and A, starting at right shoulder, pick up and k100 (100, 105, 110) sts around neck edge, including 20 (20, 22, 26) sts from Front neck holder.

Place marker and work 7 rnds in Twisted Rib. BO in pattern.

STRIPED SWEATER

Play hard. Laugh long. Good times.

In addition to its bold stripes, this sweater is notable for the decorative three-needle bind offs that are used to join the shoulders and attach the sleeves. The hand-dyed yarn features subtle variations of color, providing a fluid counterpoint to the strong horizontal lines of the stripes.

Sizes

XS (S, M, L, XL)

Finished chest circumference: 40 (43, 46, 49, 52)" [101.5 (109, 117, 124.5, 132) cm]

Length: $24^1/_4$ (25, $26^1/_4$, $26^1/_4$, $27^1/_4$)" [61.5, 63.5, 66.5, 66.5, 69) cm]

Materials

- Araucania Nature Wool Chunky (100% wool; 131 yds [119 m] per 100 g skein) in the following colors:

    4 (5, 5, 6, 6) skeins 101 Red (A)
    4 (5, 5, 5, 6) skeins 114 Yellow Green (B)

- US size 10 [6 mm] needles
- US size 9 [5.5 mm] needles
- US size 9 [5.5 mm] circular needle, 16" [40 cm] long
- Stitch holders or waste yarn
- Tapestry needle

Gauge

16 sts and 21 rows = 4" [10 cm] in St st on size 10 [6 mm] needles

Special Techniques

RIB PATTERN

Row 1 (WS): P2, (k1, p2) to end.

Row 2 (RS): K2, (p1, k2) to end.

Repeat these 2 rows for Rib Pattern.

STRIPE SEQUENCE FOR BODY

Starting with a RS row, work 11 rows in color B, then 11 rows in color A, working in St st throughout.

STRIPE SEQUENCE FOR SLEEVES

Starting with a RS row, work 6 rows in color B, then 6 rows in color A, working in St st throughout.

> Nature Wool Chunky is a hand-dyed yarn with no dye lot, so there may be significant color variation from skein to skein. To keep the colors blended, work with two skeins of a color at the same time as follows: knit two rows with the first skein, then two rows with the second skein, and so on. Or you could just knit with one skein at a time, letting the colors do what they will. It's your call.

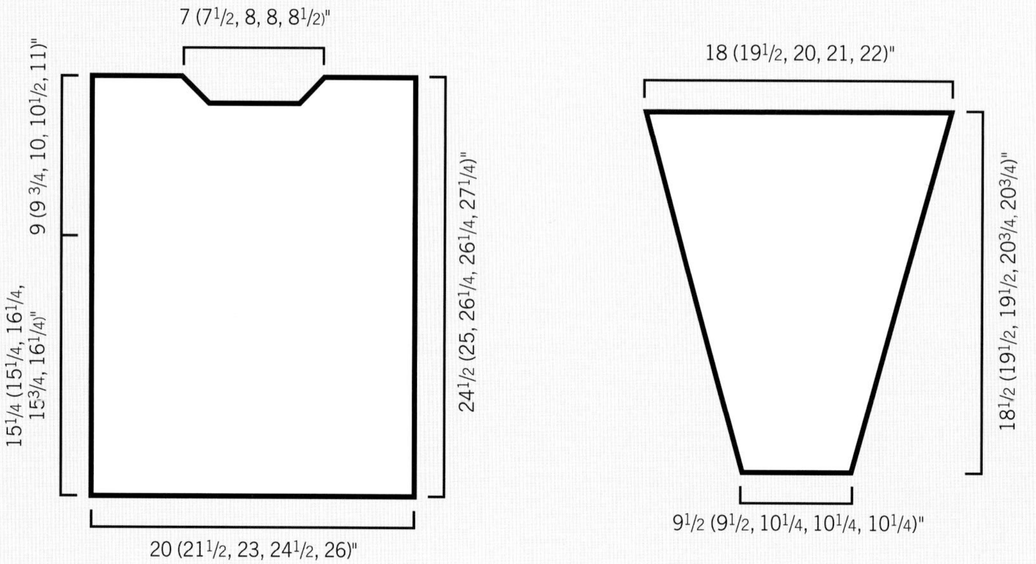
7 (7 1/2, 8, 8, 8 1/2)"
9 (9 3/4, 10, 10 1/2, 11)"
15 1/4 (15 1/4, 16 1/4, 15 3/4, 16 1/4)"
24 1/2 (25, 26 1/4, 26 1/4, 27 1/4)"
20 (21 1/2, 23, 24 1/2, 26)"
18 (19 1/2, 20, 21, 22)"
18 1/2 (19 1/2, 19 1/2, 20 3/4, 20 3/4)"
9 1/2 (9 1/2, 10 1/4, 10 1/4, 10 1/4)"

Directions

BACK

With size 9 [5.5 mm] needles and A, CO 80 (86, 92, 98, 104) sts. Work 7 rows in Rib Pattern.

Sizes S and XL [109 and 132 cm] only: Work another 4 rows with A in St st, starting with a k row.

All sizes: Change to size 10 [6 mm] needles and begin Stripe Sequence for Body until Back measures about 24 1/4 (25, 26 1/4, 26 1/4, 27 1/4)" [61.5 (63.5, 66.5, 66.5, 69) cm] from cast on, ending with a completed stripe in B (B, A, A, A).

Sizes XS and S [101.5 and 109 cm] only: Work 1 row in A.

All sizes: Place first 26 (28, 30, 33, 35) sts on stitch holder or waste yarn, next 28 (30, 32, 32, 34) sts on another holder or waste yarn, last 26 (28, 30, 33, 35) sts on another holder or waste yarn.

FRONT

Work as for Back until Front measures 20 3/4 (21 1/2, 22 3/4, 22 3/4, 23 3/4)" [52.5 (54.5, 58, 58, 60.5) cm], ending with a WS row completed.

SHAPE NECK

K32 (35, 38, 41, 43), join second skein and BO center 16 (16, 16, 16, 18) sts, k to end.

Working both sides at once, p 1 row. Dec at neck edge on next row as follows (RS): K to 4 sts from neck edge on first side, k2tog, k2; on second side, k2, ssk, k to end. Dec as established on every following RS row 5 (6, 7, 7, 7) times more—26 (28, 30, 33, 35) sts each side.

Work even until Front measures the same as Back to shoulders, ending with a completed stripe in B (B, A, A, A).

Sizes XS and S [101.5 and 109 cm] only: Work 1 row in A.

All sizes: Place remaining shoulder sts on holder or waste yarn.

SLEEVES

With size 9 [5.5 mm] needles and A, CO 38 (38, 41, 41, 41) sts. Work 7 rows in Rib Pattern.

Change to size 10 [6 mm] needles and begin Stripe Sequence for Sleeves. At the same time, when sleeve measures $1^1/2$" [4 cm] from cast on, begin sleeve shaping as follows:

Maintaining stripe sequence as established, inc 1 st at each end of next RS row and every follow-ing 4th row 7 (13, 13, 16, 22) times more, then every 6th row 9 (6, 6, 5, 1) times—72 (78, 81, 85, 89) sts.

Work even until sleeve measures $18^1/2$ ($19^1/2$, $19^1/2$, $20^3/4$, $20^3/4$) [47 (49.5, 49.5, 53, 53) cm], ending with a completed stripe in B (A, A, B, B).

Sizes XS, L, and XL [101.5, 124.5, and 132 cm] only: Work 1 row in A.

All sizes: Place sts on holder or waste yarn.

FINISHING

Join shoulder seams as follows: With WS together, using A, join each shoulder with three-needle bind off. When working the BO, have the back of the sweater facing you, and work the first shoulder BO from the outer shoulder to the neck edge. Work the second shoulder from the neck edge to the outer shoulder. Working this way will give you symmetrical BOs at each shoulder.

See page 19 for more information on working the decorative three-needle bind off.

JOIN SLEEVES

Place markers 9 ($9^3/4$, 10, $10^1/2$, 11)" [23 (25, 25.5, 26.5, 28) cm] on either side of shoulder seams.

With size 10 [6 mm] needles and A, pick up and k72 (78, 81, 85, 89) sts between markers.

With WS of sleeve and body together, the body of the sweater facing you, and using color A, join sleeve to body with three-needle bind off.

Sew side and sleeve seams.

NECKBAND

With size 9 [5.5 mm] circular needle and A, start-ing at right shoulder, pick up and k72 (75, 75, 78, 78) sts around neckline. Place marker at beginning of rnd, and work 6 rnds of k2, p1 rib. BO in rib.

RETRO VEST

Retro fit, vintage colors. Sure to get you noticed.

Three options, ranging from subtle to bold. Each employs the same slip stitch pattern, the difference being the number of colors used. This vest is meant to fit close, for a look that is tailored and very modern.

Sizes

Finished chest circumference: 38 (40, 42, 44, 46, 48, 50, 51$\frac{1}{2}$)" [96.5 (101.5, 106.5, 112, 117, 122, 127, 131) cm]

Length: 22$\frac{3}{4}$ (23$\frac{1}{2}$, 24$\frac{1}{4}$, 24$\frac{1}{2}$, 25$\frac{1}{2}$, 26$\frac{1}{4}$, 26$\frac{1}{2}$, 27$\frac{1}{2}$)" [58 (59.5, 61.5, 62, 65, 66.5, 67.5, 70) cm]

Materials

- Rowan Wool Cotton (50% merino wool, 50% cotton; 123 yards, [112 m] per 50 g skein) in the following colors:

  For one-color version (shown at left on page 78):
  8 (9, 10, 10, 11, 12, 13, 14) skeins 963 Smalt (A)

  For two-color version (shown at right on page 78):
  5 (5, 5, 6, 6, 7, 7, 7) skeins 907 Deepest Olive (A)
  4 (4, 5, 5, 5, 6, 6, 7) skeins 930 Riviera (B)

  For four-color version (shown on facing page):
  5 (5, 5, 6, 6, 7, 7, 7) skeins 956 Coffee Rich (A)
  2 (2, 2, 2, 2, 2, 3, 3) skeins 933 Violet (B)
  2 (2, 2, 2, 2, 2, 3, 3) skeins 952 Hiss (C)
  2 (2, 2, 2, 2, 2, 3, 3) skeins 929 Dream (D)

  (Another four-color version in 956 Coffee Rich (A), 962 Pumpkin (B), 929 Dream (C), and 966 Chestnut (D) is shown on page 102.)

- US size 4 [3.5 mm] needles
- US size 2 [2.75 mm] circular needle, 16" [40 cm] long
- Stitch markers
- Stitch holder
- Tapestry needle

Gauge

24 sts and 32 rows = 4" [10 cm] in St st on size 4 [3.5 mm] needles

27 sts and 42 rows = 4" [10 cm] in Main Pattern on size 4 [3.5 mm] needles

Special Techniques

RIB PATTERN

Row 1 (WS): P2, (k1, p1) to last st, p1.

Row 2 (RS): K2, (p1, k1) to last st, k1.

Repeat these 2 rows for Rib Pattern.

MAIN PATTERN

This is the basic pattern, if done in a single color.

Rows 1 and 3 (WS): P.

Row 2 (RS): K2, (sl 1 pwise wyib, k1) to last st, k1.

Row 4: K3, (sl 1pwise wyib, k1) to last 2 sts, k2.

Repeat these 4 rows for Main Pattern in one color.

To work Main Pattern in two colors:

Row 1 (WS): With A, p.

Row 2 (RS): With B, k2, (sl 1 pwise wyib, k1) to last st, k1.

Row 3: With B, p.

Row 4: With A, k3, (sl 1 pwise wyib, k1) to last 2 sts, k2.

Repeat these 4 rows for Main Pattern in two colors.

To work Main Pattern in four colors:

Row 1 (WS): With A, p.

Row 2 (RS): With B, k2, (sl 1 pwise wyib, k1) to last st, k1.

Row 3: With B, p.

Row 4: With A, k3, (sl 1 pwise wyib, k1) to last 2 sts, k2.

Row 5: With A, p.

Row 6: With C, k2, (sl 1 pwise wyib, k1) to last st, k1.

Row 7: With C, p.

Row 8: With A, k3, (sl 1 pwise wyib, k1) to last 2 sts, k2.

Row 9: With A, p.

Row 10: With D, k2, (sl 1 pwise wyib, k1) to last st, k1.

Row 11: With D, p.

Row 12: With A, k3, (sl 1 pwise wyib, k1) to last 2 sts, k2.

Repeat these 12 rows for Main Pattern in four colors.

> While the slip stitch pattern is not difficult in itself, it can be tricky to track the pattern while simultaneously working the armhole and neck shaping. Study the pattern carefully as you work the body, so you have a good handle on it when you begin the shaping.

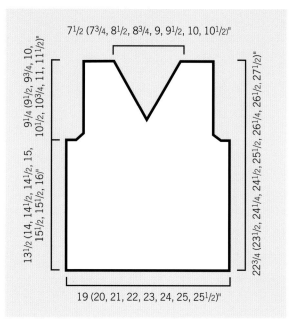

$7^{1}/2$ ($7^{3}/4$, $8^{1}/2$, $8^{3}/4$, 9, $9^{1}/2$, 10, $10^{1}/2$)"

$9^{1}/4$ ($9^{1}/2$, $9^{3}/4$, 10, $10^{1}/2$, $10^{3}/4$, 11, $11^{1}/2$)"

$13^{1}/2$ (14, $14^{1}/2$, $14^{1}/2$, 15, $15^{1}/2$, $15^{1}/2$, 16)"

$22^{3}/4$ ($23^{1}/2$, $24^{1}/4$, $24^{1}/4$, $25^{1}/2$, $26^{1}/4$, $26^{1}/4$, $27^{1}/2$)"

19 (20, 21, 22, 23, 24, 25, $25^{1}/2$)"

Directions

BACK

With size 2 [2.75 mm] circular needles and A, CO 129 (135, 143, 149, 155, 163, 169, 175) sts. Do not join.

Work in Rib Pattern for 6 (6, 6, 6, 8, 8, 8, 8) rows.

Change to size 4 [3.5 mm] needles and begin Main Pattern, working color sequence of choice. Work in Main Pattern until Back measures $13^{1}/2$ (14, $14^{1}/2$, $14^{1}/2$, 15, $15^{1}/2$, $15^{1}/2$, 16)" [34.5 (35.5, 37, 37, 38, 39.5, 39.5, 40.5) cm], ending with a WS row completed.

> Omit the slip stitch pattern when working the stitches to be bound off. Instead, knit these stitches on RS rows, and purl them on WS rows. Working the bind-off stitches in slip stitch looks untidy, and could make the bind off too tight. After binding off, the remainder of the row should be worked in pattern.

SHAPE ARMHOLES

(Maintain pattern throughout.)

All sizes: BO 7 sts at beginning of next 2 rows. BO 4 sts at beginning of next 2 rows—107 (113, 121, 127, 133, 141, 147, 153) sts.

Next row (RS): Dec 1 st at each armhole edge as follows: K1, ssk, work in pattern to last 3 sts, k2tog, k1. Dec as established on every following RS row 10 (11, 12, 13, 14, 16, 17, 18) times more—85 (89, 95, 99, 103, 107, 111, 115) sts. Work even in pattern until vest measures $22^3/4$ ($23^1/2$, $24^1/4$, $24^1/2$, $25^1/2$, $26^1/4$, $26^1/2$, $27^1/2$)" [58 (59.5, 61.5, 62, 65, 66.5, 67.5, 70) cm] from cast on, ending with a WS row worked with A completed. With A, BO in knit.

> **When working the armhole and neck decreases simultaneously, it can be very helpful to track your decreases on paper.**

FRONT

Work as for Back until armhole measures $1^1/2$ ($1^3/4$, $1^3/4$, 2, 2, 2, $2^1/4$, $2^1/2$)" [4 (4.5, 4.5, 5, 5, 5, 5.5, 6.5) cm] from first bind off, ending with a WS row completed.

With RS facing, count your sts, and place a marker in the center st of the row.

Work to center st (remembering to dec at armhole); place center st and remaining sts on holder. Turn and work 1 WS row.

SHAPE LEFT FRONT NECK

Next row (RS): Continuing with armhole shaping as established, work to last 3 sts, k2tog, k1. Dec in this manner at neck edge on every RS row until you

have worked a total of 25 (26, 28, 29, 31, 32, 33, 35) neck decs—17 (18, 19, 20, 20, 21, 22, 22) sts.

Work even in pattern until Left Front measures same as Back to shoulders, ending with a WS row worked in A. With A, BO in knit.

SHAPE RIGHT FRONT NECK

Place remaining sts back on needle.

Starting with a RS row, resume pattern as established, remembering to resume the armhole shaping as well. After this row, place the center st back on a holder.

On next RS row, begin neckline shaping, working as follows: K1, ssk, work to end of row.

Complete Right Front to match Left Front.

FINISHING

Sew shoulder and side seams.

Armhole bands: With A and size 2 [2.75 mm] circular needle, pick up and k 162 (166, 168, 172, 180, 184, 188, 196) sts around armhole. Place marker at beginning of round. Work in k1, p1 rib for 5 (5, 5, 5, 7, 7, 7, 7) rnds. BO in rib.

> It is necessary to pick up an even number of sts along the right and left front necklines—this ensures that the center front stitch from the holder will be a knit stitch when doing the neck ribbing. However, if you need to pick up a couple more or less sts than the numbers given here, that should be okay. Just make sure you have an even number of stitches along these edges.
>
> The back neck pick up should be an odd number. This will make your grand total of picked-up stitches an even number, which is correct for working k1, p1 rib in the round.

NECKBAND

With A and size 2 [2.75 mm] circular needle, starting at left shoulder, pick up and k60 (60, 62, 62, 66, 68, 68, 70) sts along left front neckline, k center st from holder, pick up and k60 (60, 62, 62, 66, 68, 68, 70) sts along right front neckline, pick up and k51 (53, 57, 59, 63, 65, 67, 71) sts along back neck—172 (174, 182, 184, 196, 202, 204, 212) sts. Place marker at beginning of rnd.

Next rnd: Work in k1, p1 rib to 1 st before center front st, sl next 2 sts together kwise, k1, p2sso, resume k1, p1 rib and work to end of rnd.

Repeat last rnd 4 (4, 4, 4, 6, 6, 6, 6) times more. BO in established rib, including the center front double dec.

Weave in ends.

COLORBLOCK SCARF

Solid. Stable. Enduring style.

Visible seaming running the length of the scarf makes construction details a key element in this design. Each half of the scarf is cast on along the long edge and worked to the center; the halves are then joined with a three-needle bind off.

Size
4" x 60" [10 x 152.5 cm]

Materials
- Debbie Bliss Cashemerino Astrakhan (60% merino wool, 30% microfiber, 10% cashmere; 76 yds [70 m] per 50 g skein) in the following colors:

  1 skein 08 Lichen (A)
  2 skeins 04 Brown (B)
  1 skein 13 Plum (C)

  (Another version in 06 Brick (A), 02 Slate (B), 04 Brown (C) is shown on page 114.)

- US size 6 [4 mm] circular needle, 24" [60 cm] or longer
- Second US size 6 [4 mm] circular needle, 24" [60 cm] or longer (used when working three-needle bind off)

You can get away with this second set being size 4 or 5 [3.5 or 3.75 mm]; just be sure to use them to hold the stitches only. Don't knit with them!

- 2 safety pins

Gauge
18 sts and 32 rows = 4" [10 cm] in garter st

Note
When changing colors, yarn is always wrapped at the back of the work as you are looking at it at that moment. This means that the wraps will show on both sides of the completed design. See page 15 for more information on intarsia techniques.

Directions
FIRST SIDE

With A, CO 156 sts. With B, CO 112 sts onto the same needle—268 sts. Turn work.

Row 1: K112 sts in B, k156 sts in A, wrapping yarns at color change.

Row 2: K156 sts in A, k112 sts in B, wrapping yarns at color change.

Repeat rows 1 and 2 until piece measures 2" [5 cm], ending with row 2. At the end of the final row, attach a safety pin to the side facing you.

Leave sts on needle and set aside. If you don't have two size 6 [4 mm] circular needles, but are using a size 4 or 5 [3.5 or 3.75 mm] for your second set, transfer these sts to that smaller needle now.

SECOND SIDE

With C, CO 156 sts. With B, CO 112 sts onto the same needle—268 sts. Turn work.

Row 1: K112 sts in B, k156 sts in C, wrapping yarns at color change.

Row 2: K156 sts in C, k112 sts in B, wrapping yarns at color change.

Repeat rows 1 and 2 until piece measures 2" [5 cm], ending with row 2 completed. At the end of the final row, attach a safety pin to the side facing you.

Leave sts on needle and set aside.

FINISHING

Join sides with three-needle bind off (see page 19), working so that the pinned sides are facing out.

It doesn't matter which color you use for this seam.

Weave in ends.

GO ANYWHERE GLOVES

Warmth with intrigue. What's your mission?

The twisted knit pattern used for these gloves adds visual interest while also making a sturdier fabric. Included are options for open-fingered and two-color fingerless versions, as well as simple but effective color work (see Options on page 85).

Sizes

S (M, L, XL)

Finished hand circumference: $6^1/2$ ($7^1/2$, $8^1/2$, $9^1/2$)" [16.5 (19, 21.5, 24) cm]

> I think gloves fit best when they are made to your hand measurement or slightly smaller. So if your hand measures 9" [23 cm] around (measuring the widest part of the palm, just under the fingers), I suggest making the $8^1/2$" [21.5 cm] glove. My hand measures $7^1/2$" [19 cm], and I can wear the smallest size here quite comfortably.

Materials

- Koigu (100% wool; 175 yds [159 m] per 50 g skein) in the following colors:

  For standard gloves (shown on facing page):
  2 (2, 2, 2) skeins KPM P521

  For open-fingered gloves (shown in orange on page 86):
  1 (2, 2, 2) skeins KPM 1110

  For two-color fingerless gloves (shown in green on page 86):
  1 (1, 2, 2) skeins KPM 2340S (A)
  1 (1, 1, 1) skein KPPPM P506 (B)

- US size 2 [2.75 mm] double-pointed needles
- US size 3 [3.25 mm] double-pointed needles
- Stitch markers
- Waste yarn

Gauge

30 sts and 40 rows = 4" [10 cm] in Twisted Stockinette on size 3 [3.25 mm] needles

Special Techniques

TWISTED RIB

Rnd 1: (K2, p1) around.

Rnd 2: (K2 tbl, p1) around.

Repeat these 2 rnds for Twisted Rib.

TWISTED STOCKINETTE

Rnd 1: K.

Rnd 2: K all sts tbl.

Repeat these 2 rnds for Twisted Stockinette.

Directions for Standard Gloves

(If you are making open-fingered or two-color fingerless gloves, review the notes in Options on page 85 before you begin.)

CUFF

With size 2 [2.75 mm] dpn, CO 48 (54, 63, 72) sts. Join into the round, placing marker at the beginning of the round. Work in Twisted Rib for 2" [5 cm].

Next rnd: Begin Twisted Stockinette. At the same time, inc 0 (2, 1, 0) sts evenly spaced—48 (56, 64, 72) sts.

Work 2 more rnds.

HAND AND THUMB GUSSET

Work in Twisted Stockinette throughout.

Change to size 3 [3.25 mm] dpn and work 1 rnd.

Next rnd: (K1, kfb) twice, k to end.

Work 3 rnds even.

Next rnd: K1, kfb, k3, kfb, k to end.

Work 3 rnds even.

Next rnd: K1, kfb, k5, kfb, k to end.

Continue as established, alternating an inc rnd with 3 plain rnds, and working 2 more sts between incs with each subsequent inc round, until you complete the "k1, kfb, k13 (15, 17, 19), kfb" rnd.

Next rnd: K2, place next 16 (18, 20, 22) sts on waste yarn (these will become the thumb), CO 2 sts with the backward loop method (see page 9), placing a marker between the cast-on sts—48 (56, 64, 72) sts. This is now the beginning of the round (you can remove the original beginning-of-round marker). K 1 rnd.**

Work in Twisted Stockinette for 13 (15, 17, 19) rnds.

INDEX FINGER

K8 (9, 10, 11), place next 32 (38, 44, 50) sts on waste yarn, CO 3 sts, k remaining 8 (9, 10, 11) sts—19 (21, 23, 25) index finger sts.

Work in Twisted Stockinette until finger measures $2^1/4$ ($2^3/4$, $3^1/4$, $3^1/2$)" [5.5 (7, 8.5, 9) cm], or about $1/4$" [0.5 cm] less than desired length, ending with rnd 2.

Next rnd: (K1, k2tog) around, ending with k1 (0, 2, 1)—13 (14, 16, 17) sts.

Next rnd: K all sts tbl.

Next rnd: K2tog around. Sizes S and XL only: End k3tog over last 3 sts—6 (7, 8, 8) sts.

Break yarn, thread tail through tapestry needle, draw through sts, and fasten off.

MIDDLE FINGER

Place first 6 (7, 8, 9) sts from waste yarn on 3 dpn. K these 6 (7, 8, 9) sts, CO 3 sts, place last 6 (7, 8, 9) sts from waste yarn on another dpn and k these sts. Pick up and k 3 sts along the CO sts from the index finger—18 (20, 22, 24) sts for the middle finger.

Work in Twisted Stockinette until finger measures $2^1/2$ (3, $3^1/2$, $3^3/4$)" [6.5 (7.5, 9, 9.5) cm], or about a $1/4$" [0.5 cm] less than desired length, ending with rnd 2.

Next rnd: (K1, k2tog) around, ending with k0 (2, 1, 0)—12 (14, 15, 16) sts.

Next rnd: K all sts tbl.

Next rnd: K2tog around. Size L only: End k3tog over last 3 sts—6 (7, 7, 8) sts.

Break yarn, thread tail through tapestry needle, draw through sts, and fasten off.

RING FINGER

Place first 5 (6, 7, 8) sts from waste yarn on dpn. K these 5 (6, 7, 8) sts, CO 3 sts, place last 5 (6, 7, 8) sts from waste yarn on another dpn and k these sts. Pick up and k 3 sts along the CO sts from the middle finger—16 (18, 20, 22) sts for the ring finger.

Work in Twisted Stockinette until finger is $2^1/4$ $(2^3/4, 3^1/4, 3^1/2)$" [5.5 (7, 8.5, 9) cm], or about $1/4$" [0.5 cm] less than desired length, ending with rnd 2.

Next rnd: (K1, k2tog) around, ending with k1 (0, 2, 1)—11 (12, 14, 15) sts.

Next rnd: K all sts tbl.

Next rnd: K2tog around. Sizes S and XL only: End k3tog over last 3 sts—5 (6, 7, 7) sts.

Break yarn, thread tail through tapestry needle, draw through sts, and fasten off.

PINKY

Divide remaining 10 (12, 14, 16) sts over 2 dpn and k them. Pick up and k 4 sts along the CO sts from the ring finger—14 (16, 18, 20) sts for the pinky.

Work in Twisted Stockinette until pinky is $1^3/4$ $(2^1/4, 2^3/4, 3)$" [4.5 (5.5, 7, 7.5) cm], or about $1/4$" [0.5 cm] less than desired length, ending with rnd 2.

Next rnd: (K1, k2tog) around, ending with k2 (1, 0, 2)—10 (11, 12, 14) sts.

Next rnd: K all sts tbl.

Next rnd: K2tog around. Size M only: End k3tog over last 3 sts—5 (5, 6, 7) sts.

Break yarn, thread tail through tapestry needle, draw through sts, and fasten off.

THUMB

Place 16 (18, 20, 22) thumb sts back on dpn.

Rejoin yarn and k thumb sts, resuming Twisted Stockinette pattern, then pick up and k 4 sts where sts were CO above thumb—20 (22, 24, 26) sts.

Work in Twisted Stockinette until thumb measures 2 (2, $2^1/2$, $2^3/4$)" [5 (5, 6.5, 7) cm], or about $1/4$" [0.5 cm] less than desired length, ending with rnd 2.

Next rnd: (K1, k2tog) around, ending with k2 (1, 0, 2)—14 (15, 16, 18) sts.

Next rnd: K all sts tbl.

Next rnd: K2tog around. Size M only: End k3tog over last 3 sts—7 (7, 8, 9) sts.

Break yarn, thread tail through tapestry needle, draw through sts, and fasten off.

Options

OPEN-FINGERED GLOVES

Work thumb and each finger as for Standard Gloves for 1" to $1^3/4$" [2.5 to 4.5 cm], depending on whether you want short or long fingers. BO in k1, p1 rib.

TWO-COLOR FINGERLESS GLOVES

Cuff

With size 2 [2.75 mm] dpn, CO with A, and work cuff as for Standard Gloves.

Hand

Continue as for Standard Gloves, alternating 1 rnd A and 1 rnd B. Work this way for the remainder of the glove.

Note: When you CO over the thumb sts and reposition the beginning-of-round marker, break the yarn not in use and rejoin it at the new beginning of the round.

Work as for Standard Gloves to **. Work in Twisted Stockinette for 9 (11, 13, 15) rnds, or about $1/2$" [1 cm] less than desired length. Change to size 2 [2.75 mm] needles and work $1/2$" [1 cm] in Twisted Rib, dec 0 (2, 1, 0) sts evenly spaced on the first rnd—48 (54, 63, 72) sts.

BO in k1, p1 rib.

Thumb: Place 16 (18, 20, 22) thumb sts back on size 2 [2.75 mm] dpn.

Rejoin yarn and k these sts, resuming Twisted Stockinette pattern, then pick up and k 4 sts where sts were CO above thumb—20 (22, 24, 26) sts.

K 2 rounds, inc (dec, —, dec) by 1 (1, —, 2) sts on the first rnd—21 (21, 24, 24) sts.

Work $1/2$" [0.5 cm] in Twisted Rib. BO in k1, p1 rib.

The Fingerless Gloves can be made in one color, of course. Or you can apply the two-color technique to the Standard Gloves or Open-Fingered Gloves.

Glove-Making Tips

There are enough tips and tricks for knitting gloves to warrant entire books on the subject (and indeed such books exist). I can't list them all here, but below are a few hints that may improve your glove-making experience.

For gloves that will be worn in snow or very cold weather, consider knitting the cuffs longer than given in the pattern.

It's likely that you will have a hole on either side of the stitches picked up for the fingers. I close up these holes while weaving in the tail of the yarn joined for knitting the finger. Another option is to pick up an extra stitch in the places where the holes appear, then decrease on the next round to reduce the number of stitches to the required number.

Wider fingers can be accommodated by casting on or picking up an extra stitch or two between fingers. You will have to make slight adjustments to the shaping at the fingertip if you add these extra stitches.

If you find your knitting loosens when knitting the fingers (not uncommon when working a small number of stitches on double-pointed needles), consider working the fingers on needles one size smaller than those used for the rest of the hand.

SLEEVELESS HOODIE

Active, sporty, casual. Travels from the courts to cafés with ease.

Intarsia stripes and color blocking invigorate this sleeveless hoodie. Wear it over a simple tee or layered over a long-sleeve shirt and under a jacket for year-round versatility.

Sizes

XS (S, M, L, XL)

Finished chest circumference: $38^1/2$ (41, 44, $47^1/2$, 50)" [98 (104, 112, 120.5, 127) cm]

Length: $22^1/2$ (24, $24^1/2$, $25^3/4$, 26)" [57 (61, 62, 65.5, 66) cm]

Materials

- Karabella Yarns Aurora 8 (100% merino wool; 98 yds [90 m] per 50 g skein) in the following colors:

    7 (8, 8, 9, 10) skeins 139 (MC)
    3 (4, 4, 4, 4) skeins 16 (CC)

- US size 7 [4.5 mm] circular needle, 24" [60 cm] or longer

- US size 7 [4.5 mm] circular needle, 16" [40 cm] long

- Stitch holders

- Tapestry needle

Gauge

18 sts and 26 rows = 4" [10 cm] in St st

Special Techniques

RIB PATTERN

Row 1 (WS): P2, (k1, p1) to last st, p1.

Row 2 (RS): K.

Repeat these 2 rows for Rib Pattern.

RIB PATTERN FOR NECK EDGE

Row 1 (WS): K1, (p1, k1) twice.

Row 2 (RS): K.

Repeat these 2 rows for Rib Pattern for Neck Edge.

RIB PATTERN FOR HOOD

Row 1 (WS): K1, (p1, k1) twice, p to last 5 sts, k1, (p1, k1) twice.

Row 2 (RS): K.

Repeat these 2 rows for Rib Pattern for Hood.

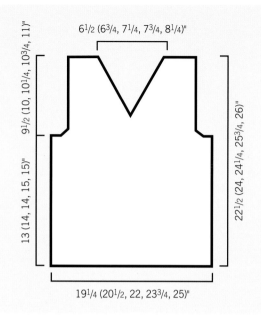

6½ (6¾, 7¼, 7¾, 8¼)"

9½ (10, 10¼, 10¾, 11)"

13 (14, 14, 15, 15)"

22½ (24, 24¼, 25¾, 26)"

19¼ (20½, 22, 23¾, 25)"

Directions

BACK

With longer circular needle, CO 5 sts in CC, 77 (83, 89, 97, 103) sts in MC, 5 sts in CC (the 5 CC sts at the beginning and end of the row should be cast on from separate skeins of yarn)—87 (93, 99, 107, 113) sts CO total. Do not join, but work back and forth in rows.

Work 5 rows in Rib Pattern, working first and last 5 sts with CC and center sts with MC. (See *Intarsia* on page 15.)

Starting with a RS row, work in St st until Back measures 13 (14, 14, 15, 15)" [33 (35.5, 35.5, 38, 38) cm], maintaining color blocking as established, and ending with a WS row completed.

SHAPE ARMHOLES

BO 5 sts at beginning of next 2 rows—77 (83, 89, 97, 103) sts. This will eliminate the CC stripes; the rest of the shaping will be worked with MC only.

Dec 1 st at each end of next row as follows (RS): K2, ssk, k to last 4 sts, k2tog, k2. Dec as established on every following RS row 9 (10, 11, 12, 13) times more—57 (61, 65, 71, 75) sts.

Work even until armhole measures 8½ (9, 9¼, 9¾, 10)" [21.5 (23, 23.5, 25, 25.5) cm], ending with a WS row completed. Break MC.

Join CC and work 6 more rows in St st.

Next row: BO first 14 (15, 16, 18, 19) sts, k across center 29 (31, 33, 35, 37) sts and place these sts on holder, BO remaining 14 (15, 16, 18, 19) sts.

FRONT

Work as for Back until armhole shaping is completed.

On next RS row, divide for left and right neck as follows:

K40 (42, 44, 47, 49). These are the left front sts. Place remaining 17 (19, 21, 24, 26) sts on holder.

LEFT FRONT

Continue in St st over 40 (42, 44, 47, 49) left front sts, working the 5 sts at the neck edge in Rib Pattern for Neck Edge.

Work as established until armhole measures 8½ (9, 9¼, 9¾, 10)" [21.5 (23, 23.5, 25, 25.5) cm], ending with a WS row completed. Break MC.

Join CC and continue in pattern for another 6 rows.

Next row (RS): BO 14 (15, 16, 18, 19) sts. Place remaining 26 (27, 28, 29, 30) sts on holder.

RIGHT FRONT

Starting with a WS row, join MC and p across 17 (19, 21, 24, 26) sts from holder. Then pick up and p23 sts along inside of left front, picking up from the back of the purl bumps (see photo below)—40 (42, 44, 47, 49) sts.

Continue in St st over 40 (42, 44, 47, 49) right front sts, working the 5 sts at the neck edge in Rib Pattern for Neck Edge.

Work as established until armhole measures $8^{1}/2$ (9, $9^{1}/4$, $9^{3}/4$, 10)" [21.5 (23, 23.5, 25, 25.5), ending with a WS row completed. Do not turn work. Break MC.

With WS facing, slide sts back to the right needle tip, join CC, and p to end of row.

Work 5 more rows in CC as follows:

Rows 1, 3 and 5: P1 (k1, p1) twice, k to end.

Rows 2 and 4: P.

Next row (WS): BO 14 (15, 16, 18, 19) sts, place remaining 26 (27, 28, 29, 30) sts on holder.

FINISHING

Sew shoulder seams and side seams.

ARMHOLE BANDS

With shorter circular needle and CC, pick up and k102 (106, 110, 114, 118) sts around armholes.

Rnds 1, 3, and 5: (P1, k1) around.

Rnds 2 and 4: K.

Rnd 6: BO in p.

HOOD

Place sts from left front, back, and right front holders onto longer circular needle—81 (85, 89, 93, 97) hood sts.

With RS facing, join CC and k across sts.

Work in St st, keeping first and last 5 sts of row in Rib Pattern for Hood, until hood measures 15" [38 cm], ending with a WS row completed.

Next row (RS): K, dec by 1 st—80 (84, 88, 92, 96) sts.

Divide remaining hood sts evenly over 2 needles: 40 (42, 44, 46, 48) sts per needle. With RS together, join with three-needle BO.

Weave in ends.

Pick up stitches through the back of the purl bumps

SPORTY PULLOVER

The sweater that takes you anywhere.

A timeless style for men. Rather than the usual rib, this sweater features a unique yarn-over variation. Color blocking on the sleeve adds a sporty element, and the deep V-neck lends the design a casual, comfortable ease.

Sizes

S (M, L, XL)

Finished chest circumference: 40 (44, 47^1/$_2$, 51^1/$_2$)" [101.5 (112, 120.5, 131) cm]

Length: 23^1/$_2$ (25, 26^1/$_2$, 27^1/$_4$)" [60 (63.5, 67.5, 69) cm]

Materials

- Elsebeth Lavold Cable Cotton (100% cotton; 93 yds [85 m] per 50 g skein) in the following colors:

    13 (15, 17, 19) skeins color 12 (A)
    1 (1, 1, 1) skein color 14 (B)
    1 (1, 2, 2) skeins color 02 (C)

- US size 7 [4.5 mm] needles

- US size 7 [4.5 mm] circular needle, 16" [40 cm] long

- Tapestry needle

Gauge

21 sts and 27 rows = 4" [10 cm] in Main Pattern

17 sts and 25 rows = 4" [10 cm] in St st

Special Techniques

RIB PATTERN

Row 1 (WS): P2, (k1, p4) to last 4 sts, k1, p2.

Row 2 (RS): K4, (sl 1 pwise, k1, YO, psso the k1 and YO, k3) to last st, k1.

Repeat these 2 rows for Rib Pattern.

MAIN PATTERN

Row 1 (WS): P.

Row 2 (RS): K4, (sl 1 pwise, k1, YO, psso the k1 and YO, k3) to last st, k1.

Repeat these 2 rows for Main Pattern.

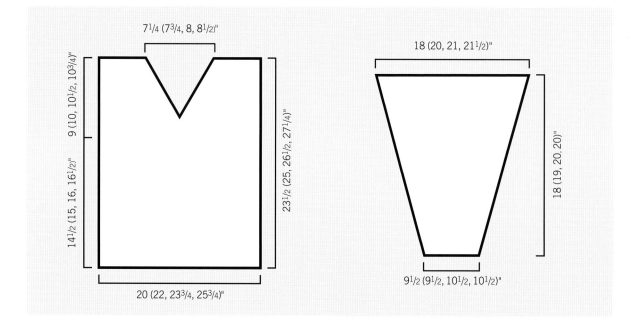

Directions

BACK

With A, CO 105 (115, 125, 135) sts.

Work in Rib Pattern for 6 rows.

Work in Main Pattern until Back measures 23^1/$_2$ (25, 26^1/$_2$, 27^1/$_4$)", ending with a WS row completed. BO in k.

FRONT

Work as for Back until Front measures 15^3/$_4$ (16^3/$_4$, 17^3/$_4$, 18^3/$_4$)" [40 (42.5, 45, 47.5) cm] from cast on, ending with a WS row completed.

SHAPE NECK

Continuing with pattern as established, begin neck shaping as follows: Work first 53 (58, 63, 68) sts, then place 53rd (58th, 63rd, 68th) st on holder, join second skein and work to end of row.

Working both sides of neck at once, p 1 WS row.

Next row: Dec at neck edges as follows: Work in patt to 4 sts from neck edge, k2tog, k2; on second neck edge, k2, ssk, work to end. Dec as established on every following RS row until you have worked a total of 17 (19, 21, 22) decs at each neck edge—35 (38, 41, 45) sts each side.

Work even until Front measures same as Back to shoulders, ending with a WS row. BO in k.

SLEEVES

With A, CO 50 (50, 55, 55) sts.

Work in Rib Pattern for 6 rows.

Begin Main Pattern. Inc 1 st at each end of next RS row, then every following 4th row 9 (23, 20, 23) times, then every 6th row 12 (4, 7, 5) times—94 (106, 111, 113) sts.

At the same time, work sleeve stripes as follows: When sleeve measures 12 (12$^1/_2$, 13, 13)" [30.5 (32, 33, 33) cm], with next row a WS row, change to B. Work in B for 4 rows.

Change to C and work in C for 16 rows.

Change to B and work in B for 4 rows.

Work remainder of sleeve in A.

Work even until sleeve measures 18 (19, 20, 20)" [45.5 (48.5, 51, 51) cm], ending with a WS row completed. BO in k.

FINISHING

Sew shoulder seams.

Sew sleeves into place.

Sew side and sleeve seams.

> It is necessary to pick up an even number of stitches along the right and left front necklines—this ensures that the center front stitch from the holder will be worked as a knit when doing the neck ribbing. However, if you need to pick up a couple more or less stitches than the numbers given here, that should be okay. Just make sure you have an even number of stitches along these edges.
>
> The back neck pick up should be an odd number. This will make your grand total of picked-up stitches even, which is correct for working k1, p1 rib in the round.

NECKBAND

With circular needle and A, starting at left shoulder, pick up and k40 (42, 46, 46) sts along left front neckline, k center st from holder, pick up and k40 (42, 46, 46) sts along right front neckline, pick up and k35 (39, 43, 45) sts along back neck—116 (124, 136, 138) sts. Place marker at beginning of rnd.

Next rnd: Work in k1, p1 rib to 1 st before center front st, sl next 2 sts together kwise, k1, p2sso, resume k1, p1 rib and work to end of rnd.

Repeat the last rnd 4 times more. BO in established rib, including the center front double dec.

Weave in ends.

CABLED HAT AND SCARF

Versatile luxury. Dress up your jeans or soften your suit.

Cables and asymmetrical blocks of seed stitch combine to create a look that is both classic and contemporary. The wool-silk yarn is lightweight and elegant, but also warm and durable.

Size

HAT
Finished circumference: $21^1/2$" [54.5 cm]

SCARF
$5^1/2$" x 60" [14 x 152.5 cm]

Materials

- 2 skeins Tess' Designer Yarns Silk and Ivory (50% silk, 50% wool; 665 yds [605 m] per 150 g skein) in Coffee Bean

FOR HAT

- US size 4 [3.5 mm] circular needle, 16" [40 cm] long
- US size 5 [3.75 mm] circular needle, 16" [40 cm] long
- US size 5 [3.75 mm] double-pointed needles
- Cable needle
- Stitch marker
- Tapestry needle

FOR SCARF

- US size 4 [3.5 mm] needles
- US size 5 [3.75 mm] needles

- Cable needle
- Tapestry needle

Notes

Yarn is worked double stranded (two strands held together as one) throughout (see page 5).

Yarn quantity given is enough to make both projects. The hat takes just under one skein. If making both, make the hat first, then use all the remaining yarn to make the scarf.

Gauge

24 sts and 32 rounds = 4" [10 cm] in St st on size 5 [3.75 mm] needles with two strands of yarn held together

Special Techniques

CABLE 5 FRONT (C5F)
Sl next 5 sts to cn and hold in front, k next 5 sts, k 5 sts from cn.

SCARF BORDER PATTERN
Rows 1, 3, and 5: (K1, p1) across.

Rows 2, 4, and 6: (P1, k1) across.

Repeat these 6 rows for Scarf Border Pattern.

Directions

HAT

Using size 4 [3.5 mm] circular needle and two strands of yarn held together, CO 120 sts. Join into the round, being careful not to twist, and place marker at beginning of rnd.

Work in k1, p1 rib for 1¹/₂" [4 cm].

Change to size 5 [3.75 mm] circular needle and work set-up rnds as follows:

Rnds 1 and 5: (K1, p1) 7 times, k1, [k10, (p2, k2) 7 times, p2] twice, k10, (p1, k1) 7 times, p1.

Rnds 2, 4, and 6: (P1, k1) 7 times, p1, k to last 15 sts, (k1, p1) 7 times, k1.

Rnds 3 and 7: (K1, p1) 7 times, k1, [k10, (k2, p2) 7 times, k2] twice, k10, (p1, k1) 7 times, p1.

Rnd 8: (P1, k1) 7 times, p1, (C5F, k30) twice, C5F, (k1, p1) 7 times, k1.

After working these 8 set-up rnds, work main pattern as follows:

Rnds 1, 5, 9, and 13: (K1, p1) 7 times, k1, [k10, (p2, k2) 7 times, p2] twice, k10, (p1, k1) 7 times, p1.

Rnds 2, 4, 6, 8, 10, and 12: (P1, k1) 7 times, p1, k to last 15 sts, (k1, p1) 7 times, k1.

Rnds 3, 7, and 11: (K1, p1) 7 times, k1, [k10, (k2, p2) 7 times, k2] twice, k10, (p1, k1) 7 times, p1.

Rnd 14: (P1, k1) 7 times, p1, (C5F, k30) twice, C5F, (k1, p1) 7 times, k1.

Rnds 15, 19, 23, and 27: (K1, p1) 7 times, k1, [k10, (k2, p2) 7 times, k2] twice, k10, (p1, k1) 7 times, p1.

Rnds 16, 18, 20, 22, 24, and 26: (P1, k1) 7 times, p1, k to last 15 sts, (k1, p1) 7 times, k1.

Rnds 17, 21, and 25: (K1, p1) 7 times, k1, [k10, (p2, k2) 7 times, p2] twice, k10, (p1, k1) 7 times, p1.

Rnd 28: (P1, k1) 7 times, p1, (C5F, k30) twice, C5F, (k1, p1) 7 times, k1.

Work rnds 1–10 of main pattern once more, then begin crown shaping, changing to dpn when necessary.

CROWN SHAPING

Rnd 11: (K1, p1) 7 times, [k2tog, k8, ssk, k1, (p2, k2) 6 times, p2, k1] twice, k2tog, k8, ssk, (k1, p1) 7 times—114 sts.

Rnd 12: (P1, k1) 7 times, k to last 14 sts, (p1, k1) 7 times.

Rnd 13: (K1, p1) 6 times, k1, [k2tog, k8, ssk, (k2, p2) 6 times, k2] twice, k2tog, k8, ssk, (p1, k1) 6 times, p1—108 sts.

Rnd 14: (P1, k1) 6 times, p1, (C5F, k26) twice, C5F, (k1, p1) 6 times, k1.

Rnd 15: (K1, p1) 6 times, [k2tog, k8, ssk, p1, (k2, p2) 5 times, k2, p1] twice, k2tog, k8, ssk, (k1, p1) 6 times—102 sts.

Rnd 16: (P1, k1) 6 times, k to last 12 sts, (p1, k1) 6 times.

Rnd 17: (K1, p1) 5 times, k1, [k2tog, k8, ssk, (p2, k2) 5 times, p2] twice, k2tog, k8, ssk, (p1, k1) 5 times, p1—96 sts.

Rnd 18: (P1, k1) 5 times, p1, k to last 11 sts, (k1, p1) 5 times, k1.

Rnd 19: (K1, p1) 5 times, [k2tog, k8, ssk, k1,(p2, k2) 4 times, p2, k1] twice, k2tog, k8, ssk, (k1, p1) 5 times—90 sts.

Rnd 20: (P1, k1) 5 times, k to last 10 sts, (p1, k1) 5 times.

Rnd 21: (K1, p1) 4 times, k1, [k2tog, k8, ssk, (k2, p2) 4 times, k2] twice, k2tog, k8, ssk, (p1, k1) 4 times, p1—84 sts.

Rnd 22: (P1, k1) 4 times, p1, k to last 9 sts, (k1, p1) 4 times, k1.

Rnd 23: (K1, p1) 4 times, [k2tog, k8, ssk, p1, (k2, p2) 3 times, k2, p1] twice, k2tog, k8, ssk, (k1, p1) 4 times—78 sts.

Rnd 24: (P1, k1) 4 times, k to last 8 sts, (p1, k1) 4 times.

Rnd 25: (K1, p1) 3 times, k1, [k2tog, k8, ssk, (p2, k2) 3 times, p2] twice, k2tog, k8, ssk, (p1, k1) 3 times, p1—72 sts.

Rnd 26: (P1, k1) 3 times, p1, k to last 7 sts, (k1, p1) 3 times, k1.

Rnd 27: (K1, p1) 3 times, [k2tog, k8, ssk, k1 (p2, k2) twice, p2, k1] twice, k2tog, k8, ssk, (k1, p1) 3 times—66 sts.

Rnd 28: (P1, k1) 3 times, (C5F, k12) twice, C5F, (p1, k1) 3 times.

Rnd 29: (K1, p1) twice, k1, [k2tog, k8, ssk, (k2, p2) twice, k2] twice, k2tog, k8, ssk, (p1, k1) twice, p1—60 sts.

Rnd 30: (P1, k1) twice, (k2tog, k8, ssk, k8) twice, k2tog, k8, ssk, (p1, k1) twice—54 sts.

Rnd 31: K1, p1, k1, (k2tog, k8, ssk, k2, p2, k2) twice, k2tog, k8, ssk, p1, k1, p1—48 sts.

Rnd 32: P1, k1, (k2tog, k8, ssk, k4) twice, k2tog, k8, ssk, p1, k1—42 sts.

Rnd 33: K1, (k2tog, k8, ssk, k2) twice, k2tog, k8, ssk, p1—36 sts.

Rnd 34: (K2tog, k8, ssk) around—30 sts.

Rnd 35: (Ssk, k6, k2tog) around—24 sts.

Rnd 36: (Ssk, k4, k2tog) around—18 sts.

Rnd 37: (Ssk, k2, k2tog) around—12 sts.

Break yarn, thread through tapestry needle, and draw through remaining sts.

Weave in ends.

SCARF

With size 4 [3.5 mm] needle and two strands of yarn held together, CO 34 sts.

Work through rows 1–6 of Scarf Border Pattern.

Change to size 5 [3.75 mm] needle, and work set-up rows for main pattern as follows:

Rows 1 and 5 (WS): (K1, p1) 4 times, p10, (k2, p2) 4 times.

Rows 2, 4 and 6 (RS): K26, (p1, k1) 4 times.

Rows 3 and 7: (K1, p1) 4 times, p10, (p2, k2) 4 times.

Row 8: K16, C5F, (p1, k1) 4 times.

After working these 8 set-up rows, work main pattern as follows:

Rows 1, 5, 9, and 13: (K1, p1) 4 times, p10, (k2, p2) 4 times.

Rows 2, 4, 6, 8, 10, and 12: K26, (p1, k1) 4 times.

Rows 3, 7, and 11: (K1, p1) 4 times, p10, (p2, k2) 4 times.

Row 14: K16, C5F, (p1, k1) 4 times.

Rows 15, 19, 23, and 27: (K1, p1) 4 times, p10, (p2, k2) 4 times.

Rows 16, 18, 20, 22, 24, and 26: K26, (p1, k1) 4 times.

Rows 17, 21, and 25: (K1, p1) 4 times, p10, (k2, p2) 4 times.

Row 28: K16, C5F, (p1, k1) 4 times.

Repeat rows 1–28 until scarf is approximately 60" [152.5 cm] long, ending with row 6 or row 20 completed.

Change to size 4 [3.5 mm] needles and work Scarf Border Pattern, binding off on row 6.

Weave in ends.

MODERN ARAN SWEATER

A classic, simplified for modern times.

This sweater was created to show off the subtle texture of the organic cotton yarn it's knit from, with a simple cable at the front chest as a focal point. Worked from the top down, it can easily be adjusted to be longer or shorter in the body and sleeves.

Sizes

S (M, L, XL)

Finished chest circumference: 40^1/$_2$ (44, 48, 52)" [103 (112, 122, 132) cm]

Length: 23^1/$_2$ (25, 27, 28^1/$_4$)" [59.5 (63.5, 68.5, 68.5, 72) cm]

Materials

- 4 (4, 5, 5) skeins Joseph Galler, Inc., Inca Cotton (100% organic cotton; 325 yds [296 m] per 227 g skein) in Ur

  (Another version in Oz is shown on page 104.)

- US size 8 [5 mm] circular needle, between 24" and 32" [60 and 80 cm] long

- US size 8 [5 mm] circular needle, 16" [40 cm] long

- US size 8 [5 mm] double-pointed needles

- 5 stitch markers (4 markers in one color, 5th marker in another color)

- 2 split ring markers

- Cable needle

- Waste yarn

- Row counter (optional, but helps in tracking the cable panel rounds)

Gauge

17 sts and 24 rows = 4" [10 cm] in St st

Special Techniques

CABLE PANEL

Worked over 26 sts.

Rnd 1: K9, sl next 4 sts onto cn and hold in front, k4, k4 from cn, k9.

Rnds 2–8: K.

Rnd 9: (Sl next 4 sts onto cn and hold in front, k4, k4 sts from cn, k1) twice, sl next 4 sts onto cn and hold in front, k4, k4 sts from cn.

Rnds 10–16: K.

Rnd 17: K9, sl next 4 sts onto cn and hold in front, k4, k4 sts from cn, k9.

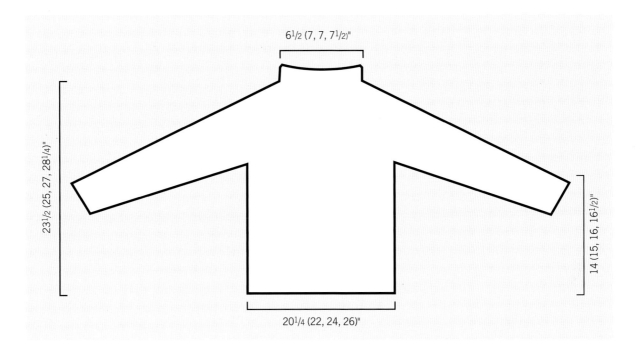

6½ (7, 7, 7½)"

23½ (25, 27, 28¼)"

14 (15, 16, 16½)"

20¼ (22, 24, 26)"

Directions

YOKE

With 16" [40 cm] circular needle, CO 54 (56, 56, 58) sts. Do not join.

Row 1 (WS): P3, pm, p10 (10, 10, 10), pm, p28 (30, 30, 32), pm, p10 (10, 10, 10), pm, p3. Use the 4 matching markers here.

Row 2 (RS): Kfb twice, k1, kfb, *k to 2 sts before next marker, kfb, k1, kfb; rep from * to last 2 sts, kfb, k1.

Row 3: P.

Row 4 (inc row): Kfb, *k to 2 sts before next marker, kfb, k1, kfb; rep from * to last 2 sts, kfb, k1.

Repeat rows 3 and 4, 4 times more, until there are 40 (42, 42, 44) sts between the second and third markers, ending with row 4 completed.

Do not turn work at the end of this row.

Using the backward loop method (see page 9), cast on 10 (12, 12, 14) sts onto the right needle tip, placing the odd colored marker between the 5th (6th, 6th, 7th) and 6th (7th, 7th, 8th) cast-on stitches to mark the beginning of the round— 124 (128, 128, 132) sts. Join work into the round.

Next rnd: K.

RAGLAN INCREASES

Inc rnd: *K to 2 sts before marker, kfb, k1, kfb; rep from * 3 more times, k to end of rnd. Be sure to increase only at the 4 increase markers, not at the odd colored start of rnd marker!

Next rnd: K.

Repeat these 2 rnds for the raglan increase, changing to the longer circular needle when appropriate.

At the same time, when front measures 3" [7.5 cm] from center front neck cast on, after completing an inc rnd, mark off cable panel as follows: Work next plain k rnd to a couple of sts past the 4th increase marker; count out 13 sts from either side of the start of rnd marker, slipping a split ring marker onto the needle after the 13th st on either side of marker. You should have the 26 center front sts marked off. These 26 sts will be the cable panel. The right split ring marker is now the beginning of the rnd (you may remove the original start of rnd marker).

Continuing to work raglan increases as established, work rnds 1–17 of Cable Panel.

After completing the Cable Panel, continue with raglan increases as established until there are 82 (90, 98, 104) sts between the back markers, 64 (70, 78, 82) sts for each sleeve, ending with a plain k rnd—27 (30, 34, 36) inc rnds worked from cast on.

Divide for body and sleeves, removing all raglan markers as you work:

K to first marker, place next 64 (70, 78, 82) sts on waste yarn, CO 4 (4, 4, 6) sts onto the right tip of the needle, k to next marker, place next 64 (70, 78, 82) sts on waste yarn, backward loop CO 4 (4, 4, 6) sts onto the right tip of the needle (see page 9), k to end of rnd—172 (188, 204, 220) body sts.

BODY

Work even on the body sts until Body measures 14 (14^1/$_2$, 15^1/$_2$, 16)" [35.5 (37, 39.5, 40.5) cm] from underarm, or until it is ^{1}/$_2$" [1 cm] short of your desired length.

BORDER

Rnds 1 and 3: (K2, p2) around.

Rnd 2: (P2, k2) around.

Rnd 4: BO in p2, k2 rib.

SLEEVES

Place sleeve sts from waste yarn onto 16" [40 cm] circular needle. Pick up and k4 (4, 4, 6) sts at underarm, placing a marker between the second and third picked-up sts—68 (74, 82, 88) sts. K to end of rnd. K4 (4, 6, 6) rnds even.

Next rnd: K1, sl 1, k1, psso, k to last 3 sts, k2tog, k1. Dec as established on every following 8th (7th, 6th, 5th) round 11 (13, 17, 20) times more—44 (46, 46, 46) sts.

Work even until sleeve measures 18 (19, 20, 20^{1}/$_{2}$)" [45.5 (48.5, 51, 52) cm] from underarm.

BO in k2, p2 rib.

NECKBAND

With 16" [40 cm] circular needle, starting at back right raglan line, pick up and k 28 (30, 30, 32) sts along back neck, 10 (10, 10, 10) sts along left shoulder, 13 sts along left neck slope, 10 (12, 12, 14) sts along center front, 13 sts along right neck slope, 10 (10, 10, 10) sts along right shoulder—84 (88, 88, 92) sts. Place marker for beginning of rnd.

Next rnd: (K2, p2) around.

Next rnd: (P2, k2) around.

Work even in St st for 1" [2.5 cm].

BO in k2, p2 rib.

MODERN FANA HAT

From the trails to the clubs. Be seen. Look great.

The "Fana" design of checks and stars originates on the west coast of Norway. The traditional Fana hat is knit in two colors and worked as a continuous tube, without any decreasing, then gathered at the crown and topped off with a pom-pom. I have modified the design to incorporate many colors, and have added crown decreasing for a smoother fit. I kept the contrast color ribbed hem, turned with a picot edge and left unsewn (to avoid a seam line across the forehead).

A picot edge is a fold line for turned hems made by alternating yarn overs with knit 2 together decreases. Used in both men's and women's garments, it's a very common element in Norwegian knitting.

Size
Finished circumference: $21^1/2$" [54.5 cm]

Materials
- Jamieson's Shetland Spindrift (100% Shetland wool; 115 yds [105 m] per 25 g skein) in the following colors:

  1 skein 540 Coral (A)
  1 skein 526 Spice (B)
  1 skein 235 Grouse (C)
  1 skein 772 Vertigris (D)
  1 skein 478 Amber (E)

- US size 2 [2.75 mm] circular needle, 16" [40 cm] long
- US size 3 [3.25 mm] circular needle, 16" [40 cm] long
- US size 3 [3.25 mm] double-pointed needles
- Stitch marker
- Tapestry needle

Gauge
28 sts and 32 rows = 4" [10 cm] in chart pattern on size 3 [3.25 mm] needles

Directions
With size 2 [2.75 mm] circular needle and A, CO 154 sts. Join in the round, being careful not to twist, and place marker at beginning of round.

Work in k1, p1 rib for 2" [5 cm].

Next rnd (picot rnd for hem): (YO, k2tog) around.

Change to size 3 [3.25 mm] circular needle and work rnds 1–17 of Star chart (see top chart on page 108).

Begin Check chart (see bottom chart on page 108), decreasing 4 sts evenly spaced on rnd 2—150 sts.

Work through rnd 39 of Check chart.

CROWN DECREASES

Change to dpn when there are too few stitches to work on the circular needle.

Next rnd: With A, (k3, sl 2 tog kwise, k1, p2sso) around—100 sts.

Change to C.

Next rnd: (K8, k2tog) around—90 sts.

Next rnd: (K7, k2tog) around—80 sts.

Next rnd: (K6, k2tog) around—70 sts.

Continue in this manner, working 1 fewer st between decs on each subsequent rnd, until you complete the (k1, k2tog) rnd.

Next rnd: K2tog around—10 sts. Break yarn, thread through tapestry needle, and draw through remaining sts. Fasten off.

Weave in ends.

Fold rib border to inside of hat and block into place.

Modern Fana Hat Charts

☐ Coral (A)
◼ Spice (B)
◼ Grouse (C)
☐ Vertigris (D)
☐ Amber (E)

STAR

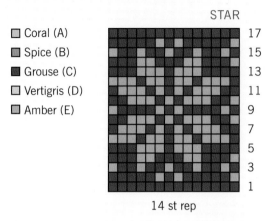

14 st rep

Knit in color shown.

Charts are worked in the round; all sts are knit all rounds; all rounds start at right side of chart.

CHECK

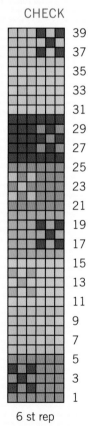

6 st rep

MODERN FANA SCARF

Eye-catching style.

Inspired by the colors in the Modern Fana Hat (see page 106), this scarf coordinates without being too matchy.

The striped section of the scarf is knit in a simple rib variation; stitches are then picked up along the edges for the two halves of the lining, which are joined with a three-needle bind off.

Size
Finished scarf: $5^1/4$" x 55" [13.5 x 140 cm]

Materials
- Jamieson's Shetland Spindrift (100% Shetland wool; 115 yds [105 m] per 25 g skein) in the following colors:

    2 skeins 235 Grouse (A)
    2 skeins 526 Spice (B)
    1 skein 540 Coral (C)
    1 skein 772 Vertigris (D)
    1 skein 478 Amber (E)

- US size 3 [3.25 mm] needles
- 2 US size 3 [3.25 mm] circular needles, 24" [60 cm] or longer
- Tapestry needle

Gauge
28 sts and 32 rows = 4" [10 cm] in St st

Directions

With size 3 [3.25 mm] needles and A, CO 37 sts.

Begin stripe sequence as shown in chart (at right).

Repeat chart until scarf measures about 55"
[140 cm]. BO in pattern on an A stripe.

LINING

With A and one circular needle, pick up and
k3 sts for every 4 rows along long edge of scarf.
Make a note of how many stitches you picked
up, so you can pick up the same number on the
second side.

Starting with a p row, work in St st, slipping the
first st of every row pwise, until lining measures
half the width of scarf. End with a k row. Leave
sts on needle.

With B and the second circular needle, work second half of lining same as first on the other edge
of scarf. With RS facing, join 2 halves of lining
with three-needle bind off (see page 19).

Weave in ends.

Modern Fana Scarf chart

Even-numbered rows
are RS rows.

☐ Knit on RS, purl on WS,
   in color shown

☐ Purl on RS, knit on WS,
   in color shown

■ Grouse (A)
■ Spice (B)
☐ Coral (C)
☐ Vertigris (D)
■ Amber (E)

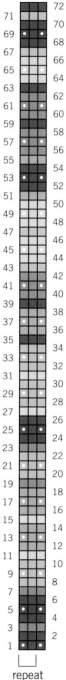

repeat

VINTAGE HELMET

Old-school knitting. Modern world vibe.

If you've ever looked at a pattern book from the 1940s, you've probably seen some version of a knitted "helmet." The version given here is true to the vintage model, but I have updated the construction to eliminate several seams, and added an option for longer front and back plates for extra warmth (see notes on page 107).

Size

One size fits just about everyone.

Materials

- Rowan Wool Cotton (50% merino wool, 50% cotton; 123 yds [112 m] per 50 g skein) in the following colors:

    For basic version (shown in blue on page 112):
    3 skeins 955 Ship Shape

    For front and back plates version (shown in red on page 112):
    4 skeins 911 Rich

- US size 2 [2.75 mm] circular needle, 16" [40 cm] long
- US size 4 [3.5 mm] circular needle, 16" [40 cm] long
- Stitch markers
- Stitch holders
- Safety pin
- Tapestry needle

Gauge

24 sts and 32 rows = 4" [10 cm] in St st on size 4 [3.5 mm] needles

32 sts and 32 rows = 4" [10 cm] in Twisted Rib on size 4 [3.5 mm] needles

Special Techniques

TWISTED RIB

Row 1 (WS): P1, (p2, k1) to last 3 sts, p3.

Row 2 (RS): K1, (k2tbl, p1) to last 3 sts, k2tbl, k1.

Repeat these 2 rows for Twisted Rib.

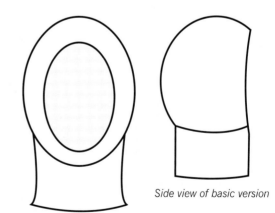

Side view of basic version

Front view of basic version

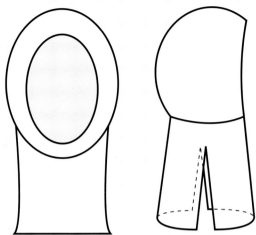

Front view of front-and-back-plates version

Side view of front-and-back-plates version

Directions

With size 2 [2.75 mm] needles, CO 160 sts. Join into a circle, placing marker at the beginning of the rnd.

Work in k1, p1 rib for 1" [2.5 cm].

Next rnd: K140, sl last 20 sts of rnd onto holder. Sl first 19 sts of rnd onto same holder—39 sts on holder, 121 sts on needle.

Change to size 4 [3.5 mm] needle and work in Twisted Rib over center 121 sts for 5^1/$_2$" [14 cm], ending with row 2 completed. Piece will measure 6^1/$_2$" [16.5 cm] from cast on. Looking at the RS of your work, place a safety pin on the left selvedge edge (this pin indicates where you pick up sts later).

BO 36 sts in pattern at the beg of the next 2 rows—49 sts.

Continue in pattern for a further 5^1/$_2$" [14 cm], ending with row 2. Do not turn work.

Slide these 49 sts onto size 2 [2.75 mm] circular needle.

With same needle and yarn, pick up and k41 sts along the selvedge edge marked with a safety pin. Work across 39 neckband sts on holder as follows: K1, (p1, k1) across; pick up and k41 sts along selvedge edge corresponding to safety pin edge; work across the initial 49 sts slid onto the size 2 [2.75 mm] needle as follows: P1, (k1, p1) across—170 sts.**

Place marker for beginning of rnd, and work in k1, p1 rib for 4" [10 cm], or until neckband reaches desired depth. BO in rib.

FINISHING

Sew the seams along the back of the helmet.

Weave in ends.

TO MAKE A HELMET WITH FRONT AND BACK PLATES

Work as above to **. Place marker for beginning of rnd, and work in k1, p1 rib for 3" [7.5 cm].

Divide for front and back plates: Work 21 sts in rib, place next 79 sts on holder.

Turn work and work across 91 sts, maintaining established rib pattern. Work in rib until back plate measures 8" [20 cm] from start of rib band, or to desired depth.

BO in rib.

With RS facing, place 79 sts from holder back onto size 2 [2.75 mm] needle, join yarn, and resume established rib pattern. Work in rib until front plate measures 8" [20 cm], or to desired depth.

BO in rib.

TOP DOWN HATS

No rules. Cast on, get going, and see what happens.

These instructions allow you to knit a hat without a pattern, without a gauge swatch, and with no planning.

These are general directions that can be modified to accommodate different yarns, stitch patterns, and so on. Once you have made a couple of basic hats, it will be easy to modify the directions to create your own unique designs (see Options on page 116).

Size

Up to you.

Materials

- Yarn of your choice; use the following samples as yardage guidelines.

  For the red hat:
  2 skeins Debbie Bliss Cashemerino Astrakhan (60% merino wool, 30% microfiber, 10% cashmere; 76 yds [70 m] per 50 g skein) in color 6

  US size 6 [4 mm] needles

  For the striped hat:
  1 skein Noro Kureyon (100% wool; 109 yds [100 m] per 50 g skein) in color 146

  US size 7 [4.5 mm] needles

  For the earflap hat:
  1 skein ShibuiKnits Highland Wool Alpaca (100% Australian wool; 227 yds [206 m] per 250 g skein) in Bark

  US size 11 [8 mm] needles

- Double-pointed and circular needles, 16" [40 cm], in a size appropriate to your selected yarn.
- Stitch marker
- Tapestry needle

Some lower borders may require a circular needle one or two sizes smaller than that used for the crown of the hat. For example, rib and seed stitch borders are often worked on needles smaller than those used for the rest of the hat. This makes the border pull in and hug the head.

Similarly, I find I knit loosely when working the increase rounds at the start of the hat, especially when working with a bulky yarn. To keep the knitting from being too loose, I use needles a size smaller than those recommended on the yarn label. Once the increasing is complete, I switch back to the recommended size.

Directions

Cast on 4 sts with dpn.

Row 1: Kfb in each st—8 sts.

Divide among 4 dpns, join into the round, place marker to mark beg of round.

Rnd 2 and all even rnds: K 1 rnd.

Rnd 3: Kfb in each st—16 sts.

Rnd 5: (Kfb, k1) around—24 sts.

Rnd 7: (Kfb, k2) around—32 sts.

Rnd 9: (Kfb, k3) around—40 sts.

Continue incs as established, alternating an inc rnd with a k rnd, and working 1 more k st between incs on each subsequent inc rnd, until hat fits head circumference.

> For bulkier yarns, or to create a flatter crown, you may want to omit some of the plain rounds at the top of the hat.

Work even to desired length, incorporating any desired edgings.

BO.

BO can be in pattern, knit, or k1, p1 rib (this is a good option if you tend to bind off tightly).

Options

TO ADD EARFLAPS

Make hat as directed above, stopping just before the bind off. Set hat aside and make earflaps.

Make 2 earflaps:

With dpn, CO 3 sts and work in I-cord (see page 15) until tie is desired length (about 12" [30.5 cm] is a good starting point for an adult hat).

> If you prefer a hat without ties, or with braided ties (see page 54), eliminate the I-cord at the start of the earflap. Instead, CO 3 sts and follow directions for either the Dot Stitch or the St st earflap.

For a Dot Stitch (similar to Seed Stitch) earflap:

Set-up row: Kfb twice, k1—5 sts.

Row 1 (WS): (K1, p1) to last st, k1.

Row 2 (RS): Kfb, k to last 2 sts, kfb, k1—7 sts.

Repeat rows 1 and 2 until you have 3–4" [7.5–10 cm] worth of sts on the needle. End with a WS row. Break yarn and leave on dpn. Make second earflap in same manner as first.

For a St st earflap:

Set up row: Kfb twice, k1—5 sts.

Row 1 (WS): P.

Row 2 (RS): Kfb, k to last 2 sts, Kfb, k1.

Repeat rows 1 and 2 until you have 3–4" [7.5–10 cm] worth of sts on the needle. End with a WS row. Break yarn and leave on dpn. Make second earflap in same manner as first.

To attach earflaps:

Earflaps should be centered at the midpoints of the hat or just slightly toward the back of the head. BO hat sts until you reach the point where the first earflap goes, then join flap to hat as follows: Holding earflap behind hat sts (both sets of sts in your left hand, with needles parallel and WS of hat and flap facing each other), join earflap to hat with three-needle bind off (see page 19). BO to where second earflap goes, join with three-needle bind off, BO remaining sts.

STRIPING TECHNIQUE FOR VARIEGATED YARNS

To make stripes out of a single colorway of variegated yarn (as shown in the striped hat on page 114), work as follows:

Divide skein into 2 balls, making sure each ball starts at a different place in the yarn's color sequence. To make the hat as shown, work 3 rnds with ball 1, then 3 rnds with ball 2. Continue to alternate in this manner.

Do not cut yarn after each change; instead, carry the yarn not in use up the inside of the hat.

You can make the stripes as wide or as narrow as you like, or you can make the stripes different widths.

Divide the skein into 3 or 4 balls for even more stripe variation.

This technique is most successful with yarns with long color runs. Variegated yarns with very short color runs won't stripe as distinctly.

TO ADD STITCH PATTERNS

Here are some stitch patterns you can incorporate into your hats. They can be used as edgings, or for the greater part of the hat. It gets a bit tricky to incorporate a pattern into the increase rounds, so you might want to work that section in St st, then switch to another stitch pattern once the shaping is completed.

Dot Stitch

(For a sample of dot stitching, see the earflap hat on page 114.)

Worked over an even number of sts.

Rnd 1: (K1, p1) around.

Rnds 2 and 4: K.

Rnd 3: (P1, k1) around.

Repeat these 4 rnds for Dot Stitch.

Seed Stitch

(This is a nubbier, more textured version of the dot stitch; not shown.)

Worked over an even number of sts.

Rnd 1: (K1, p1) around.

Rnd 2: (P1, k1) around.

Repeat these 2 rnds for Seed Stitch.

2X2 BROKEN RIB

(This is a more subtle and faster-to-work alternative to ribbing; not shown.)

Worked over multiples of 4 sts.

Rnd 1: (K2, p2) around.

Rnd 2: K.

Repeat these 2 rnds for Broken Rib.

YARN RESOURCES

Brown Sheep Company

www.brownsheep.com

(800) 826-9136

- Lamb's Pride Worsted

Jamieson's of Shetland

www.jamiesonsofshetland.co.uk/jamiesons

- Shetland Spindrift

Joseph Galler, Inc.

(800) 836-3314

- Inca Cotton

Knitting Fever

www.knittingfever.com

(516) 546-3600

- Araucania Nature Wool Chunky
- Debbie Bliss Cashmerino Astrakhan
- Elsebeth Lavold Cable Cotton
- Noro Kureyon

Koigu Wool Designs

www.koigu.com

(888) 765-WOOL

- KPM
- KPPPM

ShibuiKnits

www.shibuiknits.com

(503) 595-5898

- Highland Wool Alpaca
- Merino Alpaca
- Merino Kid
- Sock

Tess' Designer Yarns

www.tessdesigneryarns.com

(800) 321-TESS

- Silk and Ivory

Westminster Fibers/Rowan

www.knitrowan.com

- Felted Tweed
- Scottish Tweed DK
- Wool Cotton